∨ rec'd 11/09

A HEAVENLY CHRISTMAS
IN HOMETOWN

A HEAVENLY CHRISTMAS
IN HOMETOWN

SHARON K. SOUZA

WINEPRESS **WP** PUBLISHING

Packaged by WinePress Publishing, PO Box 428, Enumclaw, WA 98022. The views expressed or implied in this work do not necessarily reflect those of WinePress Publishing. The author(s) is ultimately responsible for the design, content and editorial accuracy of this work.

Scripture references are taken from the King James Version of the Bible.

ISBN 1-57921-747-8
Library of Congress Catalog Card Number: 2004092074

For
Joshua, Haleigh, Katelyn
Jacob & David
. . . and those to come . . .
with much love

Acknowledgments

Writing is a solitary craft, but it's never done in a vacuum. I'd like to thank the very special people who helped make this story come to life.

Rick, you've always kept the dream alive and I love you that much more because of it. Thank you for helping to solve the practical aspects of this and every other story I've written. I could never do it without your help. And thank you for always encouraging me, just when I need it most.

Deanne, Mindy and Brian. You are my cheerleaders, and I so love and appreciate you. Thank you for reading . . . and reading . . . and reading, and still wanting more. You'll never know how your encouragement and enthusiasm has kept me going. You are the best.

Janice, this story was birthed from one of the many creative ideas that just seem to spring from you. I'm glad I was in the right place at the right time. I hope you'll do the play . . . Of course, it could never beat . . . well, you know.

Lord Jesus, thank You for letting me write stories that bring glory to Your Name. I could do nothing without You.

One

The chamber was impressive, and that was an understatement of enormous proportion. Assembled within its ancient, hallowed walls, was a group known simply as The Committee. Its members were of the highest rank, as were their assignments. Membership was a thing to be coveted . . . in another place and time.

"The meeting will come to order," the Chairman said. He sounded his gavel, then stood to address The Committee. "As you know, that most sacred and distinctive of all human events, the time when men's hearts rejoice for the glad tidings that were delivered to them, a time, dear friends, of universal good will, is again upon the earth. I refer, of course, to Christmas. As the season unfolds, we have before us a great task—one that will require a degree of, shall I say, *finesse*." He held up a document with the case number 163408576832-P and sadly shook his head. "Another holy celebration has been challenged."

"Challenged?" asked Brother Spencer. "What on earth do they think Christmas is all about?"

"That's a good question," the Chairman said. "And we must help them arrive at the correct answer. This assignment has a rating of NI—Nearly Impossible—and could take what mankind refers to as *time*, and a great deal of it. But, there's a promotion for anyone who takes this assignment and succeeds. Now then, who will begin the nominations?"

Several hands went up, to the Chairman's delight.

"The Chair recognizes Brother Terrence."

"Thank you, Brother Chairman. It is my great pleasure and privilege to nominate one who is esteemed among us, one whose merits are too numerous to name. I refer, of course, to our dear Brother Zebedee."

"Very good, Brother Terrence. The secretary will please note Brother Zebedee's name on the board."

"Oh, dear," stammered Brother Zebedee. "I graciously acknowledge your nomination. However, as you know, I *am* first harpist in the orchestra. One could hardly pursue such an indefinite business under the circumstances."

"I see." The Chairman forced a smile in the direction of the first harpist. "The secretary will remove Brother Zebedee's name from the board."

"However, I in turn would like to nominate Sister Terese," said Brother Zebedee.

"Excellent choice!" declared the Chairman. "Make a note of that," he said to the secretary.

"Oh no," said Sister Terese, shooting out of her seat. "Like my esteemed Brother, I am indeed honored by the nomination. However . . . ."

"However?"

"I too have commitments that would prohibit me from accepting such a diffi—I mean *consuming* assignment. I am in charge of the rookies this term, you know."

"I hadn't heard," the Chairman said drolly, and motioned to the secretary again. "Strike that one, too. Brother Amos, have you a nomination?"

"I'd like to nominate Brother Horace."

"Oh, my," gasped the nominee. "I'm afraid I cannot accept."

And on it continued.

The Chairman was growing weary when another hand went up in the back of the room. It belonged to a seasoned member of The Committee whose merits were all-too-often overlooked. "There hardly seems to be anyone left to nominate, Brother Eustace, but be my guest."

"Thank you, Brother Chairman." He stood to his feet. "I know this is somewhat irregular, but I'd like to nominate . . . myself, sir."

"Yourself?" the Chairman asked. That truly was a surprise.

"Yes, sir. I'd like the assignment."

The Chairman shot the Vice Chairman a look of surprise. "Has this ever happened before?"

"Not to my knowledge. But if no one objects."

The Chairman swept a confident eye across the room then sounded his gavel. "We have a nomination," he declared. "Is there a second?" A chorus of seconds was heard. "Brother Secretary, please write Brother Eustace's name on the board. As a formality we'll put it to a vote. All in favor say aye." A chorus of ayes bounced off the chamber walls. "Opposed?" The room was at once deathly silent. "The ayes have it. Congratulations, Brother Eustace. This meeting is adjourned." The gavel sounded once again and The Committee members hurried out, before Eustace had a chance to change his mind.

"Now what did you go and do that for?" Spencer asked his friend. His voice echoed in the empty chamber. "Do you know what you've gotten yourself into?"

Eustace was silent.

"Yes, I guess you do," Spencer said with a sigh.

"It's an important assignment. I can't think of anything more challenging for the holidays."

"Or difficult."

"That too," Eustace agreed. "Well, if you'll excuse me, I have some packing to do."

"Won't you be lonely? All by yourself, I mean?"

A curious eyebrow went up. "Why do you ask?"

"You know very well why I ask," said his friend. "I can't let you go alone. But you counted on that all along, didn't you?" Spencer, a younger member of The Committee, smiled fondly at Eustace.

For a reply, Eustace returned the smile.

Spencer looked around the chamber, which was beautifully decorated in honor of the Christmas season. Maybe, if all went well, they'd complete their assignment and be back in time to celebrate with the heavenly host. "I'll clear this with the Chairman, then get some things together."

"Great. I'll meet you at your place. And, Spencer. Thanks." With all his heart he meant it.

"What on earth should I take?" Spencer thumbed through his closet. An empty bag lay open on a chair.

"I took the liberty to include a few things for you," Eustace said, holding up a small suitcase. "I hope you don't mind."

"I see we're traveling light." He replaced his own bag in the closet and took one last look around. He didn't know what to expect on this trip, but he was sure he wouldn't see anything as lovely as his home here in the

Heavenlies. "I'm ready if you are," he said, hoping the butterflies he felt in his stomach didn't show on his face.

"Then let's get started. We've a long way to go."

They'd been traveling only a short while when Eustace turned an inquisitive eye upon his young companion. "You seem a little nervous, Spence. Is something wrong?"

"I didn't want to mention it before, but, well, this is my first time to go."

"Ah. I thought it might be. Is that why you volunteered?"

"Not entirely. Well, mostly," he admitted. "What about you? Have you been, you know, *there*?"

"Yes, once. A long time ago."

A mixture of awe and apprehension crossed Spencer's face. "What was it like?"

"It's rather hard to explain unless you have some knowledge of the language. I've forgotten many of the terms, but they'll come back to me."

"How does one learn the language?"

"It's acquired very easily once you enter the atmosphere. Since you've never been, I don't suppose you have any concept of *time*?"

"I've heard about it, but I must admit it's difficult to understand. What exactly is it?"

"Let me see if I can explain. Eternity, the realm in which we exist, is without beginning or end. On earth, however, there are tiny units of measured existence called *days*. They're forever starting and stopping. One moment it's today and the next moment it's tomorrow, which becomes today all over again."

"How odd."

"Quite," Eustace said, "but humanity finds it agreeable."

"Really? Please, tell me more."

"Well, for one thing there's the existence of *night* on earth. The days I was telling you about are divided into two parts: half is day and the other half is night when it isn't day at all."

"Well, if it isn't day why do they call it day?" asked Spencer, obviously confused. "And what is night?"

Eustace tried hard to explain. "Night is the portion of day when darkness covers the earth."

"Darkness?" Spencer scratched his head. "You know, I've heard of darkness, but what exactly is it?"

Eustace searched for an answer his friend might understand. "Darkness is the opposite of light."

"The opposite of light?" Spencer repeated. "I'm afraid I can't conceive of such a thing. The whole topic is very confusing."

"I'm sure you'll catch on eventually."

"How did Earth receive you the first time you went? I assume they were astounded."

"Actually, except for a handful of shepherds, they hardly took notice."

"Hardly took notice? Truly?"

"Truly."

Spencer was shocked that such was the case, and contemplated what it should mean. "Not take notice?" he whispered to himself, while Eustace enjoyed the lull in the conversation.

Their journey was well under way and the Heavenlies were far behind. The soft, warm light to which Spencer was accustomed gave way to a cool dimness. A sense of rapid motion was evident, as their surroundings became darker and colder. No such feeling of motion existed in the Heavenlies. Movement was a state of mind rather than body. This new sensation left Spencer a little queasy.

"Just a little motion sickness," Eustace explained. "It'll soon pass."

"Is it normal?"

"Quite."

His eyes blinked involuntarily as he tried to drive away the approaching darkness. "This must be night?" His question sounded hollow in the empty atmosphere.

"It's only the beginning, my boy." Eustace's smile was lost to his companion. "In just a little while you'll understand it fully."

Spencer wondered if he'd made a terrible mistake in wanting to come. "I don't think I'll like it."

"But you'll get used to it," replied his friend.

On they journeyed, moving closer to the whirling orb hung eerily in the darkness. A feeling of heaviness settled upon them, yet the movement of their travel was unaffected.

"Why do I feel like this, Eustace? So sluggish."

"It's called weight," he explained. "You'll get used to that as well."

"I don't think I'll like that, either. How slow the human race must travel."

"Unfortunately, not slowly enough. It's life in the fast lane as they say. Rushing here, rushing there. Everyone in a hurry. Especially this time of the year. It's a jungle."

"How do you know so much about humanity?" Spencer asked.

The old angel smiled. "I read a lot."

As their journey continued, they lost sight altogether of the Heavenlies. Spencer began to feel more earthy and less angelic. "Where exactly are we going, Eustace? And when will we get out of this awful darkness? I can't see a thing."

Eustace took the orders from his pocket. Trying to focus his eyes in the dimness, he held the orders at arm's length. Still, he could hardly make them out. He placed a pair of eyeglasses on the end of his nose, and began to read.

"What on earth are those?" Spencer asked.

"They're spectacles."

"They certainly are."

"No, I mean eyeglasses. They help you see things more clearly in this veiled environment."

"Could they help me see through this awful darkness?"

"No, I'm afraid they don't work like that, Spence." Eustace smiled. "From the looks of these orders we're going to Hometown, USA. Sounds like an interesting place, don't you think?"

"It sounds interesting, but how will we ever see it? Everything looks so . . . so . . ."

"Dark."

"Exactly."

"See, my boy, you're picking up the lingo already. But don't worry, things will look different in the morning," Eustace promised.

"One can only hope."

Morning did bring welcome changes as Spencer and Eustace continued their descent. The sky was a crisp blue on the early December day, and blankets of fresh clean snow covered the ground.

Spencer looked around him with pleasure. "This is more like it. It even has the appearance of the Heavenlies. Everything is so clean and white. Is this where we're going?"

"Yes, I think so," said Eustace, referring to a map. "It looks as if we've reached our journey's end. Are you ready?"

"I'm ready."

"Then let's land."

Their feet touched Earth in a matter of moments, bringing their flight to an end. Spencer, feeling the effects of his journey and the burden of his body weight, dropped himself onto the ground for a short rest. Instantly, he was back on his feet.

"What on earth is *that*, Eustace?" He shivered for the first time in his life. "It's . . . it's . . ."

"Cold. It's called snow, Spencer. This is winter."

"It looks like home, but it sure doesn't feel like it. Snow, you say?" He reached down and picked up the white powder, which melted in the warmth of his hand. He'd expected it to feel like a cloud. It definitely did not. "How odd."

"I think we'd better get on, Spence. Hometown should be just over this hill. But first let's change into our earthly attire." Eustace opened the suitcase and removed several items. "You'll need a shirt and trousers," he said, handing the items to Spencer, "and socks and shoes." Before the words were spoken Eustace was dressed. "This jacket should be nice and warm, and a hat will just finish it off." He pulled one out of his suitcase and fitted it on his head. "What do you think?" He turned to show off his wardrobe.

"A bit strange," Spencer confessed. "How do I look?"

"Much the same, I'm afraid."

Spencer frowned as he adjusted his jacket. "It seems rather binding, but I suppose it will have to do. Shall we continue?"

"Yes, but, Spencer," Eustace said, pulling him back to Earth, "we'd better walk the rest of the way."

Two

Hometown, USA, was a lovely little hamlet, with lovely little homes, which all had clean, well-trimmed yards with whitewashed fences around each one. It had sprung up over the years around Town Square, where stood City Hall, which had the loveliest and best-trimmed grounds of the entire community. In it stood a perfectly shaped pine adorned with twinkling Christmas lights and other decorations for the holiday season. It was no wonder that Town Square was the pride of Hometown. Spencer looked with admiration upon the scene as it came into view. "I have a feeling they've misrated our assignment," he said. "No doubt we'll be home enjoying our promotion in no time."

"I hope you're right," Eustace said, but in his heart he didn't think so. "We're looking for Miss Perry's boarding house. According to our orders, we have reservations there. Do you see a sign anywhere?"

"I think it might be that house on the end." Spencer squinted as he pointed to a neat two-story building. "Yes, that's it."

"It does looks very homey, don't you think? We should be quite comfortable." Eustace knocked at the front door.

It was answered by a soft-looking woman some years past her prime. She smiled a greeting as she looked from one to the other. "Good morning," she said with a delicate voice, "can I help you gentlemen?"

"I believe you have a room for rent." Eustace tipped his hat to the lady.

"Why, yes I do, but however did you know? It only became vacant this very morning, and I haven't even put my 'VACANCY' sign in the window."

Spencer offered a pleasant smile. "May we see it?"

"The sign?" she asked.

"The room," Eustace said.

"Oh, of course." She giggled an embarrassed little laugh. "Just follow me. It's the room in the front. The one that faces Town Square. The best in the house."

She led them to a large, immaculate room that would easily accommodate the two. "This is very nice," Eustace said. "If you haven't promised it to anyone else we'd be happy to have it." His angelic smile so charmed Miss

Perry that she forgot her usual list of questions and handed over the key to her new boarders at once.

"Get settled and we'll go over our rules and regulations at dinner, the first of which is that we dine promptly at two."

All of the boarders were present when Eustace and Spencer arrived at the table. Miss Perry motioned to two empty chairs.

"I hope we aren't late," said Eustace.

"Not at all." She took her own seat at the head of the table, all joined hands, and grace was offered over the meal, as was the custom of Miss Perry's boarding house. Eustace and Spencer exchanged a look of satisfaction.

As the boarders served their plates, introductions were made on behalf of the new ones. Joshua Andrews sat to the right of Miss Perry. Being the boarder of the longest duration it was his rightful place. He was an elderly man, long retired, and held the honor of being the great grandson of the town's first mayor. He had been a boarder at Miss Perry's since his wife's passing seventeen years before.

To his right sat Walter Jeffries who was the boarder of the second longest duration. That's the way it worked at Miss Perry's. He was the town's post master and had occupied his room fourteen years.

Next was Oliver Bentley, a fine old gentleman of noble heritage, for the Bentleys had helped found Hometown. No one knew what he did besides occupy his favorite bench in Town Square Park and tell stories to any of the townsfolk who hadn't grown tired of his tales, but that earned him the title of "historian," and for that he was well respected.

Dudley Welsh sat next to Oliver. He'd been a boarder nine years and was also retired, but then most of Miss Perry's boarders were. Besides having retirement in common, the gentlemen also shared a mild infatuation for their landlady. But, they agreed that their present situation was quite agreeable and, in order to nip adverse competition squarely in the bud, merely doted from a distance.

Emery Daniels was next in line, and being a younger tenant, regarded Miss Perry with something less than amorous affection, but regarded her nonetheless. Emery was a reporter for the *Hometown Herald*, and, as tools of his trade, possessed eyes and ears that never missed a thing. As it happened, he occupied the room next to Eustace and Spencer.

"And that brings us to you two gentlemen," said Miss Perry. "Where did you say you're from?"

"We didn't," replied Spencer, to which Emery Daniels raised an eyebrow, "but it's quite a distance from here."

"You've probably never been there," Eustace added. "It's just a small place up north."

"I've been just about everywhere," boasted Emery.

"I doubt you've been *there*," Spencer said with certainty.

Oliver buttered another biscuit. "What do you fellas do for a living?"

"We're . . . investigators," said Eustace.

"Yes, that's what we are," Spencer confirmed. "We're investigators."

"Oooh, how exciting!" Miss Perry's cheeks dimpled as she smiled. "But whatever could you find to investigate in Hometown? Nothing out of the ordinary ever happens here."

"You might be surprised," Spencer said, with a hint of secrecy, but a look from Eustace silenced him at once.

"The most extraordinary thing that ever occurred here," continued Miss Perry, "was the time Martha Bradbury's kitchen blew up. Abel Caruthers, the fire chief, got stuck sliding down the pole on account of eating so many of Martha's pies. Well, as it happened, the keys to the fire truck were in Abel's pocket and no one could get to them. They had to send for a truck from Elmwood—that's seven miles west of here—but by the time it arrived, Martha's kitchen had gone up in smoke. They did save the rest of the house, at least most of it, and they managed to get Abel free, but it was weeks before Martha would even consider baking him another pie."

"How dreadful," said Eustace.

"What is it you fellas are investigating?" asked Emery. "Must be something important to take you away from your families so close to the holidays."

Eustace just smiled and nodded, doing his best to evade the question.

"You must hate to be away from your families," pressed the reporter.

"We haven't any," offered Spencer, who was silenced again by a look from Eustace.

"Are you bachelors?" asked Miss Perry. "*Both* of you?"

For an answer Spencer looked to Eustace. "Are we?"

"Most decidedly," Eustace replied.

"Why, don't you know?" Miss Perry asked Spencer with a laugh.

"You'll have to get used to Spencer. He does like to tease." Eustace shot a reproachful glance in his direction. "What delicious biscuits. Did you bake them yourself?"

"Oh, yes," said the landlady. "I do all of the cooking here." She smiled and quite forgot about Spencer. Emery Daniels, however, raised another eyebrow and wondered a great deal about the new lodgers.

"Would you care for some pie, Mr—?"

"Eustace will do."

"Well then, Eustace, would you care for some pie? I baked it fresh today."

"Thank you, Miss Perry, I'd love a piece."

"Do call me Caroline," she urged. All of the boarders raised an eyebrow then, in unison, but Miss Perry was quite oblivious as she moved toward the kitchen. "I'll only be a minute."

Eustace felt self-conscious as the gentlemen studied him with great suspicion, growing greater by the moment. The older boarders had their own reasons for their suspicions, but Emery's came from his role as reporter. His nose for news, passed down from a long line of newspaper men, could smell a headline a mile away. He shifted his gaze from one to the other and back again, and wondered what they had up their sleeves. Whatever it was, he intended to sniff it out.

Dessert, though delicious, was decidedly quiet, but Miss Perry didn't seem to notice. She provided Eustace with a second piece of pie—an unheard of event—and turned down Oliver Bentley's offer to help with dishes.

"What do you make of those two?" asked Dudley when the gentlemen—all but Eustace and Spencer—moved into the parlor for their customary cup of warm cocoa.

"I dunno," said Walter. "What do you think, Emery?"

"I think I'm going to keep an eye on them, that's what I think. And I'm going to do some investigating of my own."

"Good idea," agreed the gentlemen.

"Is there anything we can do to help?"

"As a matter of fact there is, Walter. If you could keep an eye on their mail, if they get any, we might learn where they're from. And, Oliver, you just might ask your sister to let you know if they get any calls. Being as Clara's our only telephone operator they can't get by her. We'll find out about their 'small place up north,' and when we do I plan to take a little trip and find out what they're up to."

While this meeting was under way, Spencer and Eustace put on coats, hats and scarves, and left the warmth of Miss Perry's boarding house to have a look around the town. From every angle it looked like a scene from a Currier and Ives Christmas card. The clear, blue sky looked down on mounds of white snow settled on windowsills and perched on the tops of evergreen boughs. The smell of cozy fires drifted from chimneys as smoke curled above housetops and mingled with the scent of pine. The fragrances of winter.

"What a heavenly aroma," Spencer declared. "Or should I say earthly? Whichever, it's quite delightful. What a lovely place Hometown seems to be."

"It does *seem* to be, but there's a reason we were sent here. Perhaps it's not wise to judge this book by its cover."

"I don't know, Eustace. Take a look around. I didn't know what to expect with this being my first visit, but if it's as bad as we've been led to believe do you think it could look so peaceful? Why, from one end of town to the other there's nothing but harmony. I'll say it again; I do believe we'll be home by Christmas enjoying our promotion."

Three

*T*he quiet of the winter's day was broken as Spencer and Eustace neared the church at the end of town where their walk had led them. Ever so faintly the sound of singing could be heard. As they got closer, the blended voices filtered out into the afternoon with a sound that delighted both the ear and the heart.

O come let us adore Him
Chri-ist the Lord

"Doesn't it remind you of home, Eustace?" Spencer closed his eyes and imagined himself back in the Heavenlies where the voices of angels were no doubt singing the same anthem. "I never would have thought the beauty could be duplicated on earth."

"It must be the message that gives it such a heavenly sound. Shall we go in?"

"After you," said Spencer, as he opened the door.

Inside, the music filled the empty sanctuary with such beautiful tones that Spencer couldn't resist joining in. His angelic voice rose above the others so magnificently that all others ceased. Unaware of his solo, Spencer sang with a heart of worship and adoration unlike anything the choir had ever heard. All stopped to listen, overcome by the beauty of the tones, until Eustace silenced Spencer with a nudge.

"Oh, please continue," said the director, who had turned to listen along with his choir.

"We didn't mean to disturb your practice," Eustace apologized. "My friend got carried away."

"It was lovely," the young man said with a smile, then addressed the choir. "We'll sing hymn one eighty-seven Sunday morning. Be here at the usual time." With thanks for their attendance, he dismissed them, then turned his attention to the visitors.

"I'm Tim Parsons," he said offering his hand.

"I'm Eustace and this is Spencer."

"You must be new in Hometown. I don't think I've seen you before. I know I've never *heard* you before." He turned his eye toward Spencer. "Would you be interested in joining the choir? We sure could use you."

"Are you the choir director?" asked Eustace.

"The choir director, custodian, and any other position that needs filling. In short, I'm the pastor."

"Pastor Parsons?" Spencer asked.

"Kind of funny, isn't it?"

"It's a pleasure to know you, Reverend," Eustace said.

"Oh, please, just Tim. Here." He moved to a pew. "Have a seat. So, you're new to Hometown?"

"Actually, we're just visiting," Eustace replied, taking a seat next to the pastor.

"Oh, that's too bad. We really could use Spencer in the choir. Will you be here for the pageant?" he asked, then a frown creased his brow. "That is if we have a pageant this year."

"What kind of pageant?" Eustace asked.

"Our Christmas program. It's a long-standing tradition to have a living nativity in Town Square."

"Well, how nice! Is that what you were rehearsing for? It sounded divine."

"Thank you, Spencer. Yes. It really is a magnificent affair. The whole town turns out to see the Christmas story reenacted, complete with donkey, wise men, and even the heavenly host."

"Imagine that," said Spencer with an eyebrow raised.

"But this year, rehearsal may be as far as we get. There's a new ordinance that calls for separation of church and state."

"What on earth is that?" Spencer asked.

"It simply means we can hold no religious activity at any municipal site."

"I've never heard of such a thing."

"Is there no such ordinance where you come from?"

"Certainly not!"

"How fortunate you are," Tim said with a sigh.

"If the whole town gets involved in the pageant," Spencer said, "why is there a problem? Who would complain?"

"Have you ever heard of Scrooge?"

"Well, of course," the young angel replied, "but that's another story."

"I wish it were. Unfortunately, Hometown has its very own Scrooge, by the name of Parsons. Andrew Parsons."

"A relative?"

"My uncle."

"I see." Eustace tapped his fingers on the wooden pew. "And he's insisting that this separation ordinance be enforced?"

"Exactly."

"He must have some leverage to stand up to the entire town," Spencer said. Eustace gave him an approving smile, impressed with the language Spencer was already picking up.

"He owns the lumber mill, which employs ninety percent of Hometown's work force. My uncle has never been a tolerant man, especially in matters of religion," Tim continued, "but it's gotten even worse in the last year. He says he's tired of workers 'robbing him blind' by receiving wages for religious holidays when they haven't 'worked a lick.' His words, not mine. But that's only an excuse. The real reason is that he's angry and bitter about the death of his wife, my Aunt Helen. She was a godly woman, and even though my uncle considers religion a weakness, he admired the Christian qualities that made my aunt such a fine lady. They were very close, and I know he misses her terribly."

"When did your aunt pass away?"

"Last Christmas."

Spencer seemed thoughtful for a moment. "Oh, yes, I think I remember . . ."

"Never mind, Spencer," Eustace said with a slight nudge of his elbow.

Tim gave Spencer a puzzled look, but continued. "My uncle never came to church, but when Aunt Helen became ill he started making large contributions. Last year, he alone financed the pageant. Between you and me, I think he was trying to buy her health. When she died he was very angry."

"No wonder he wants to stop the pageant."

"How did this ordinance come about?" Spencer asked.

"Shortly after my aunt's death Uncle Andrew began to press the City Council to adopt the ordinance. We'd heard all during the holidays that city after city had done so. Can you imagine such a thing in America, a land founded for the purpose of religious freedom?"

"Hardly," murmured his listeners.

"How did he convince the council members to adopt it?" asked Eustace.

"Most of them are employed by, or are closely related to employees of, the mill. They had no choice but to adopt it. I don't think anyone realized it would mean eliminating the pageant from Town Square. I certainly didn't. But as the season drew near and we began our rehearsals, Uncle Andrew reminded us of the ordinance and said there would be no pageant."

"What do you plan to do now?"

"Pray for a miracle, I guess."

"Well, that's why we're here," Spencer said with a smile, leaving Tim to wonder what he meant, and Eustace shaking his head.

A door opened just then and a young woman entered the sanctuary. "I saw the choir leave and thought you might like some coffee. Oh, I'm sorry, Tim, I thought you were alone."

"It's okay, honey. I'd like you to meet these gentlemen. Eustace and Spencer, my wife, Beverly."

"I'm happy to meet you," she said, offering her hand and a warm smile.

"The pleasure is ours," Eustace replied. He took her hand and made a slight bow. Spencer, following Eustace's example, did likewise.

"Would you join us for coffee?" Tim asked.

"Please do," added Beverly, charmed by their visitors. "It's a fresh pot. And I've made cinnamon rolls."

"We hate to impose," Eustace said.

"It's no imposition," Beverly assured them.

"In that case, we'd be happy to."

"Very happy," Spencer added. He didn't know what a cinnamon roll was, but if it was as good as Miss Perry's pie, he was anxious to try one.

They entered the parsonage through the same door Beverly had used. A short hallway led them into a warm and cozy kitchen where a delightful aroma greeted them. Beyond the kitchen a fire crackled in another cozy room lit only by the blaze.

"Tim, if you'll take our guests into the living room I'll bring in a tray. Turn on a light," she added, as the three made themselves comfortable. Eustace and Spencer took chairs near the fire, while Tim sat on one end of a sofa. He snapped on a lamp and the room was bathed in a soft, golden light. Spencer and Eustace liked the feel of the room.

Beverly set her tray on the table and served each of them coffee and a roll.

"This is wonderful," Spencer declared. "What did you call it?"

"It's just a cinnamon roll." She looked inquisitively at her guest. "Haven't you ever had one?"

"I'm sure I'd remember if I had."

She began to laugh. "I get it. You're teasing. Would you like another one?"

"I really shouldn't," he said, but took one just the same.

"And when is the pageant to be held?" Eustace asked, getting back to business.

"Christmas Eve. Three weeks from today."

"Have you tried to reason with your uncle? Surely he must know what it means to the whole town."

"There's no reasoning with Uncle Andrew. He won't see me or answer my calls."

"The truth is," Beverly said, "he's had nothing to do with Tim since his ordination."

"And very little before that," Tim added.

"Not even last year? You said he financed the pageant by himself."

"He financed it, but wouldn't come. To my knowledge he's never seen the pageant. And he's got the power to make sure no one else ever sees it again."

"It'll be such a shame if we have to cancel." Beverly put her arm through her husband's. "Raymond and Misty are looking so forward to it."

"They're our children," Tim said.

"And they both have parts in the pageant this year."

As if on cue, the two children burst through the front door, giving themselves to laughter as only children can. They were dressed in heavy winter clothing, and wore mittens and scarves to protect against the cold.

"It's snowing again!" Misty exclaimed. Her cheeks and nose were a frosty pink, and her eyes sparkled with glee. A white powder atop her knitted cap melted in the warmth of the room. "Can we stay outside and play, Mama?"

"You'd better not. It's getting awfully cold."

Spencer shivered as he remembered the icy snow.

"How about some hot cocoa and a cinnamon roll?" Beverly helped Misty out of her jacket, as her daughter's disappointed frown changed to a look of pleasure. "Is that a yes?"

Misty nodded.

"Raymond?"

"Yes, please." Raymond hung his coat on a rack, and stuck his mittens in the pockets. Misty's coat lay in a heap near the sofa.

"Hello there, young man," said Eustace. "You must be Raymond."

"Yes, sir," replied the boy. He was shy but polite, and took the hand Eustace offered.

"My name is Eustace. My friend here is Spencer. We're very pleased to meet you."

"Thank you," said Raymond.

"I understand you have a part in this year's Christmas pageant?"

He nodded and a smile lit up his face. His eyes, the softest, most transparent blue Eustace had ever seen this side of Heaven, were alive with merriment. "I get to be a shepherd," he said, "and I get to carry a real live lamb. It's from Mr. Wintzel's petting zoo, and it's really soft. Well, I think it's soft. I haven't held it yet, but it sure looks soft."

"And I get to be an angel!" cried Misty, who was not at all shy.

"An angel?" said Eustace. "Well now, that is something." And he wrapped his arms around them both. "An angel and a shepherd. Those are very important parts, you know."

The children nodded. Misty's blond curls bounced, and her eyes, the same transparent blue as her brother's, were bright and sparkling. She was seven; Raymond ten.

"Are you going to be in the pageant?" she asked Eustace. "You can be a wise man. My daddy's going to be Joseph, and Mama gets to be Mary. Do you know who Mary is?"

"Yes, I believe I do"

"When I grow up I want to be Mary," Misty said to Eustace, then looked up at Spencer who was enjoying the children's enthusiasm. A shy smile revealed dimples, and she lowered her eyes. Her father was surprised at Misty's sudden and uncharacteristic bashfulness, but Beverly's look explained it all. It was Misty's first crush.

"Do you like being an angel?" Spencer knelt down before her.

She nodded. "I don't say anything, but I get to wear wings and a halo. Raymond doesn't say anything, either," she added, not wanting to be upstaged.

"I'm sure you look beautiful in your wings and halo." He winked. "And I'm sure Raymond makes a fine shepherd."

"I think we'd better be going," said Eustace. "It's nearly dark."

"Must you leave so soon?" Beverly asked. "How about some more coffee?"

"Thank you, but we really should go." Eustace and Spencer took their coats from Tim.

"Will we see you again?" he asked.

"I'm sure of it," Eustace said, and shook his hand.

Darkness had fallen, but street lamps shed a hazy glow that lighted them on their way. Spencer already didn't mind the darkness so much, at least not when it looked like this. The scene was one of serenity.

"Town Square," said Eustace, stopping before a plaque. "'Upon this site Hometown was founded in the year of our Lord . . .'" Eustace stopped reading. "Looks like they'll have to change the plaque."

"Or maybe they should remember the importance of His birth."

Eustace patted him on the back. "You have a point there, Spence."

"What are we going to do, Eustace? Do you think there's any way to help?"

"I hope so. Undoubtedly, that's why we've come." He pulled his coat tighter around him, and they headed back toward Miss Perry's boarding house. "Tim and his family are delightful people. I'd like to see them help Hometown."

"And I'd like to see the pageant, complete with heavenly host." Spencer joyfully kicked a clump of snow and watched the hazy light reflect off the scattering flakes.

"Maybe we will. I think I'll pay a visit to Tim's uncle tomorrow. Care to go along?"

"Well now, I wouldn't miss it for the world."

Four

Andrew Parsons sat alone in the study of his rambling two-story house. A fire was kindled in the fireplace, but it offered little warmth. He studied the flames with a scowl, and shivered. "Why must it always be so blasted cold in this house?" he asked aloud.

A bell beckoned the butler to the front door where two unfamiliar, and unexpected, gentlemen waited. The younger shivered in the cold. "May I help you?" the butler asked in a voice that came from his nose.

"We'd like to see Mr. Parsons."

"May I tell him who's calling?"

"You may tell him Eustace and Spencer."

"Eustace and Spencer? Is there nothing more, sir?"

"Nothing more. Just Eustace and Spencer. We're friends of his nephew."

"I see," said the butler. "Wait here, if you please."

He tapped on the door of the study, then went in. "Two gentlemen to see you, sir."

"I'm not expecting anyone," the old man snapped. "Send them away."

"Very good, sir." The butler bowed then moved toward the door. In anticipation, he paused.

"What are their names?" The old man's words sounded like a growl.

"Mr. Eustace and Mr. Spencer, sir. They're friends of your nephew."

"My what? Oh, yes, *him*. Friends you say? What do they want to see me about?"

"They didn't say, sir. Shall I ask?"

"No. Yes. Wait a minute, Higgins. Show them into the study."

"Very good, sir."

"No doubt they've come about the pageant," he said to himself after Higgins left. "Come to plead for mercy. I'll show them mercy, all right. I'll throw them out on their ears," he said with a ghastly laugh.

"Good afternoon, Mr. Parsons," Eustace said, in a straightforward and businesslike manner.

"Who are you and what do you want?" he demanded. "Did my nephew send you? He should know better."

"No one sent us," Eustace replied. "We'd like to speak with you if we may."

"Then speak." He removed a gold watch from his vest pocket. With a stub of a thumb he lifted the cover to check the face. "And make it quick. I have *scheduled* business shortly." *That* was an outright lie.

Eustace came right to the point. "We'd like you to reconsider the pageant."

"I knew it!" he roared. "He did send you. Well, you can go right back and tell him there will be no pageant in Town Square! Do you hear me? No pageant!"

"Really, Mr. Parsons, what can it hurt?" Eustace pressed.

"It's the law, Mr. Whoever-you-are. And if my nephew doesn't like it, let him try to change it."

"We both know that would be pointless as long as you oppose it."

"That's right," he said with an ugly grin. "Money talks. Always has and always will." He looked at his watch with a frown. "Is there anything else?"

"You have the reputation of a Scrooge," blurted Spencer.

"I have, have I? Well, young man, Scrooge happens to be my hero. At least he was until he went and got sentimental! Bah humbug! Tell that to my nephew!"

"Raymond and Misty will be disappointed." Eustace attempted to reach a tender spot in the old man's heart.

"What do I care for Raymond and Misty, whoever they are." He waved a dismissive hand.

"They're your nephew's children. Awfully nice kids, and they're looking forward to the pageant. The whole town is from what I'm told."

"The whole town be hanged."

"Won't you at least think about it? For the sake of Christmas; you know, peace on earth, good will to men?"

"I don't believe in good will, and I don't believe in Christmas!"

"What *do* you believe in?" Spencer snapped.

"Hold your tongue, young man!"

"Please, Spencer," Eustace whispered.

Spencer bit his lip as Eustace faced the old man. "Mr. Parsons. As a businessman, you must understand the importance of good morale amongst your employees. The pageant means a lot to them."

"So do their paychecks. No pageant!"

"I understand you've never even seen it. I assure you—"

"Who said I've never seen it?"

"Your nephew—"

"My nephew, indeed! What does he know?" Andrew snapped down the cover of his watch. "You're out of time. Higgins will show you out." And with that, they were dismissed.

Once outside, Spencer muttered his indignation. "Bah humbug, indeed! What a cantankerous old scoundrel."

"Be careful, Spencer," Eustace warned. "Whatever he is, we mustn't be tempted to judge."

Emery Daniels, watching from behind a tree, pulled out a notebook. He made an entry in it as he mumbled to himself, "December 5, 12:10 P.M. Met with Old Man Parsons." He closed it with a snap, then said to himself, "Now what do you make of that?"

He followed at a distance, but kept Eustace and Spencer within sight. They wandered through the town, in and out of shops, all of which took full advantage of the season. Decorations were festive and merchandise plentiful to please the many shoppers, not to mention the merchants. Spencer probed, inspected and questioned. There were so many things he'd never seen before.

"Eustace, what on earth is this?" he asked, turning an item over in his hands. "And what does it do?"

Too late, Eustace saw the "LADIES WEAR" sign. "I believe it's called a girdle, Spencer. And never mind what it does." He snatched it from his friend, dropped it back on the table, and led him to another department. "I think we'll be safe here. Browse to your heart's content."

Spencer inspected items of hardware while Eustace pretended to do so. By the time they finished, Spencer had a pretty good idea of how to stock a tool box, though he had little use for one.

"Do you suppose he's ready for a rest?" asked Eustace, as they left the last shop.

"Is who ready for a rest?"

"Emery Daniels. He's followed us since we left Tim's uncle."

"You don't say," Spencer said. Eustace stopped him before he could turn to look. "Why on earth would he follow us?" His voice dropped to a whisper.

"Don't worry, he can't hear you. He's a block or two behind. I'm sure his reporter's curiosity has been roused. He can't figure us out."

Spencer started to look around again, but Eustace stopped him. "Do you think he'd like to go to the pond and watch the children skate? I think we'll find Raymond and Misty there."

"I'm sure he'd love it," Spencer said, though he hadn't the foggiest idea what a skate might be.

The children were there with a dozen skaters or more, most of whom had mastered the ice. Raymond was among the advanced, but Misty wobbled terribly. She blushed upon seeing Spencer, but determined she would do her best for her audience. Her efforts were noble, but her ankles were weak and she continued to wobble. Eustace rented skates for himself and Spencer, then took to the ice like a pro.

"Now where do you suppose he learned to do that?" Spencer asked himself, amazed. His own ankles quivered like jelly as he tottered toward the pond. Uncertainly, he stepped onto the ice. Before he had a chance to get his balance his feet came out from under him and down he went. Now it was his turn to blush, and blush he did. Raymond was beside him in a flash and helped him back on his feet.

"Keep your ankles straight and balance yourself on the blades," he said. "Like this." And showing him the way, led him once or twice around the pond. "That's better. You're doing fine."

Eustace, with Misty on his arm, glided over the ice. He steadied her when she wobbled, and soon she too was doing well. Her big blue eyes expressed her delight, and she thanked Eustace over and over again for his help.

"It's a pleasure, my dear." And truly it was; for Eustace and for Spencer, who couldn't remember when he'd had so much fun, and his memory went *way* back.

Emery made another entry in his notebook then headed for the boarding house. When he and his cohorts were assembled in the parlor he told them what he'd seen. "Somehow they're in cahoots with Old Man Parsons. That old goat cares only about his own interests. If these guys are investigators—and I have my doubts—what would they be investigating for the old man?"

"If you don't think they're investigators, what do you think they are?" asked Walter Jeffries.

"I don't know, Walt, but they're spying on something for someone and I'm gonna find out what and who, or I'll turn in my typewriter."

Just then the dinner bell rang, and Eustace and Spencer entered the house, frosty and joyful from their outing.

"We'll talk more tomorrow," whispered Emery, as they moved into the dining room.

"You're right on time." Miss Perry said. She seated herself at the table. The men followed in unison. "What have you two been up to?"

"Skating!" exclaimed Spencer. "Can you imagine?"

"Why, everybody skates around here, Mr. Spencer. It's practically required in Hometown. My, I haven't been in a month of Sundays." She sighed.

"We can remedy that," said Eustace. "The next time we take the Parsons children you'll have to go along."

"Oooh," giggled Miss Perry, "do I dare?"

"Hmph," said a gentleman or two.

Her green eyes twinkled. "I think I will."

"Don't they skate up north where you come from?" asked Emery suspiciously.

"Not that I've ever seen," Spencer replied, "but maybe we could arrange for a pond or two. What do you think, Eustace?"

"I think it's out of the question. It doesn't get cold enough."

"Up *north*, and not cold enough?" pressed Emery. "That seems a little odd."

"We have a good deal of sunshine," he explained.

"Oh, a good deal," Spencer agreed. He didn't need a look from Eustace to silence him this time. He was beginning to learn when he'd said too much.

"The Parsons children are delightful," said Miss Perry. "And what lovely parents. Pastor Parsons is a saint."

"Indeed he is," Eustace said.

"Too bad he's got such a nasty uncle," added Emery. "But, of course, you fellas wouldn't know about that."

"Well, how could they?" asked Miss Perry. "Old Mr. Parsons never goes out. He's rather like the skeleton in our community closet," she said to Eustace. "Very disagreeable. We're glad he keeps to himself."

Before Eustace could address Emery one way or the other, Miss Perry changed the topic of conversation. "I suppose you know about the pageant? What a shame we can't have it this year. I can't remember a Christmas when we didn't have the pageant."

"Couldn't they have it someplace else?" Eustace wondered.

"Yes, but where? Any place that would be big enough is all municipal property."

"I saw a sign that said Hometown Memorial Park as we came into town," said Spencer. "Why don't they have it there?"

"Mr. Spencer!" gasped the landlady. "That's our churchyard!"

"Well, that's all the better. If it belongs to the church nobody can complain."

"Spencer." Eustace beckoned him to come closer. He whispered something behind his hand.

"Dear me," he replied with a blush.

"Don't tell me you don't have churchyards up north either," cried Dudley Welsh, and they all had a good laugh at Spencer's expense.

Five

Tim's office was small but comfortable. He welcomed Eustace and Spencer who were right on time, and poured them all steaming mugs of coffee.

"Thank you for seeing us, Tim. Especially on such short notice."

"I always have time for friends," he said. "Besides, I have more time than usual on my hands these days."

"You haven't given up on the pageant, have you?" Eustace asked.

"With only two weeks until Christmas Eve and no place to have it, I don't have much choice. We'll just have a nice quiet service, maybe sing a few carols instead."

"What about all the work that's been put into it?"

"And what about Raymond and Misty?" added Spencer.

"They'll be disappointed. Everyone will. But I don't know what else to do."

"There must be some other place big enough for the pageant," Eustace said. "Someplace that isn't subject to that silly ordinance." He stood, then paced the length of the office. Both Tim and Spencer watched him, hoping that somehow he'd think of something. "What a lovely picture, Tim." He pointed to an oak-framed drawing hanging on the wall. "What's it of?"

"It's a rendering of the church we hope to build some day. It would give us a sanctuary large enough for our congregation, plenty of classrooms for Sunday school, and a separate facility for a day school. Isn't it nice?"

"Very," said Eustace with interest. "Will you build here on this site?"

"Oh, no. We have a plot of land that will accommodate us perfectly. My aunt left it to the church in her will, but my uncle is contesting it. So, we have the money to build, but until the courts decide the matter, we can't do a thing. That could take years."

"Why is he contesting it? Does he have use for the property, or does he just want to keep the church from using it?"

"Both. I told you how he feels about religion, so that's part of it. But there's more. The property is a prime chunk of land situated on the highway. He wants to build a restaurant and lodge for travelers and tourists.

It's a gold mine, Eustace. He'll fight for it, and with his money he'll probably win."

"Has he no regard for your aunt's wishes?" Spencer asked.

"Greed tends to supersede the dictates of our hearts, I'm afraid. Besides, he feels I coerced her into leaving it to the church."

"Did you?" asked Eustace.

Tim shook his head. "Aunt Helen wanted to see us build a new church with a school. It was her idea to have the rendering made. No one coerced her."

"I was sure that was the case, but I wanted to hear you say it."

"She was a great lady with a big heart. And as self-*less* as my uncle is self*ish*."

"How on earth did she end up with a man like him?" Spencer looked as if he'd tasted something bitter.

"A better question is, how on earth did he end up with a woman like her?"

"Where is this property?" Eustace asked. "Would you mind if we took a look at it?"

"Not at all. It's east of town about eleven miles. I'll draw you a map." Tim scratched the directions on a piece of paper and handed them to Eustace. "I have an appointment, so I can't go with you, but I can loan you my car."

"Oh, we'll manage. Thanks just the same."

In next to no time, Eustace and Spencer stood at the edge of the contested site. It was nestled in between two mountain peaks, blanketed with freshly fallen snow, and strategically adorned with scenic pines.

"This would make a beautiful resort," said the older angel.

"Resort?" cried Spencer. "What on earth do you mean? Tim's aunt didn't leave this for a resort. She left it for a church. And a school." Spencer frowned at his friend. "Eustace, is this atmosphere getting to you?"

"Not that I know of. I just think it would make a lovely resort. Look at those slopes. They were simply made for skiing."

"Skiing. What on earth is that?"

"It's a little like skating, only you do it on slick, polished boards attached to your boots."

Spencer gasped. "On boards? Down that mountain?"

"Would you care to try?"

"I should say not."

"I want you to picture something with me, Spencer. Night has fallen, and it's beginning to snow. You've just eaten a scrumptious dinner, and now you're relaxing before a cozy fire with a nice cup of cocoa. You feel a little drowsy."

"A little what?"

"Drowsy. Sleepy. In need of rest."

"Oh, you mean like people."

"Exactly. So you go upstairs to your comfortable room, take a nice hot shower and retire for the night. In the morning you wake fresh and invigorated. You breakfast on waffles and jam, then ride up the mountain for a day on the slopes. Doesn't it sound fun?"

"Is it really?"

"I tell you, Spencer, it's great fun. I wish the lodge were here this minute so I could show you."

"But what about the church? And the school?" He eyed his companion narrowly. "Are you getting a little worldly, Eustace? Have you forgotten why we came?"

"Of course not. A church and a school would be nice. Heaven knows they need a bigger sanctuary, but really, Spencer, do they need it *here*? A church would look quaint nestled in between these mountains, but a resort would put them to good use."

"But Eustace, Helen Parsons left *this* land for *that* church. What would she say to a resort?"

"You can ask her when we get home, Spence. Personally, I think she'd be the first to see my point."

"What exactly is your point?"

"Andrew Parsons strikes me as a man who likes to haggle. Perhaps we're here to do a little bargaining."

"I don't know what on earth you're up to, Eustace, but whatever it is, I hope it works."

Emery Daniels tightened his muffler and raised the collar on his coat. He blew into his hands, then shoved them into his pockets. His binoculars hung around his neck. From atop the ridge he could see those two "investigators" surveying Helen Parsons' property. "So that's what this is all about," he said to himself. "They're in cahoots with the old man, all right." With furrowed brow he scribbled another entry into his notebook, then headed down the other side of the slope to his waiting car.

Eustace turned and looked at the spot where Emery had stood a moment before. "We'd better *walk* back to town, Spence."

Before Spencer could argue, a car turned off the highway and pulled over a few yards in front of them.

"Care for a ride?" called Emery.

"Why, thank you, Mr. Daniels. We'd appreciate a lift."

"You're a far piece from town," said Emery, as they started on their way. He studied his passengers out of the corner of his eye.

"We're just out for a stroll," Eustace explained. "Walking is a great source of exercise."

"It's eleven miles to town," said Emery dryly.

"Lucky for us you happened along."

"What are you fellas doing out in this neck of the woods? Most times there's nothing out here but chipmunks and 'possums, but it's not likely you'll run across any this time of year."

"We were carried away by the scenery."

"Oh you were, huh? Is this so different from your place up north?"

"A little," is all Eustace would say. "And where have you been, Mr. Daniels?"

"Out looking for news."

"Amidst the chipmunks and 'possums?" Eustace grinned.

Emery gave a sidelong glance. "And a skunk or two." Silence accompanied them to the outskirts of town. "Can I drop you off at the boarding house?" Emery asked.

"If it's no trouble, we're going to the church," Eustace replied.

"No trouble. I'm going that way myself."

With thanks for the ride, Eustace and Spencer closed the car door, then stepped behind the church in the direction of Tim's office. As soon as they were out of sight Emery turned his car and headed for home. Eustace peaked around the corner just as Emery went by, then motioned for Spencer to follow him.

"I thought we were seeing Tim," he said, pointing behind him.

"That's what we wanted him to think," Eustace replied.

"And I thought he was going the other way."

"That's what he wanted us to think."

"I'm confused."

"That's okay. Just follow me."

Emery had his fellow boarders assembled in no time. Their curiosity was aroused by his manner, and every eye remained fixed on their leader.

"Guess where I found those 'investigators' this morning?" He waited until their curiosity peaked then gave them the answer. "I saw them with my own eyes staking out that property Helen Parsons left the church."

"Helen Parsons' property?" Dudley's eyes were wide with surprise.

Oliver plunked his hat onto his lap. "You don't say."

The gentlemen gaped at each other with astonished looks but, to tell the truth, they didn't know why. Walter was the first to confess his lack of understanding.

"What does it mean, Emery?" he asked with a frown.

"What does it mean? It means they're working in cahoots with Old Man Parsons, just like I said. They're making out to be bosom buddies with the preacher and his wife, warming up to their two kids like they are, when all the time they're planning to swindle the Reverend—and the church—out of that property." Emery concluded with a punctuating nod, and the meeting closed with a collective gasp.

Six

I don't think we have a leg to stand on." Eldon Baker, attorney at law, fidgeted in his chair under the gaze of his client. "No one will believe your nephew forced your late wife into changing her will. She was of sound mind, Mr. Parsons, and perfectly within her rights."

"It's your job, a job for which you're well paid, to convince the courts otherwise." He slammed his hand down on the arm of his chair. "Why would Helen do such a thing without telling me? And why would you let her?"

"It was as she wished."

"As she wished!" He scowled, then added, "Rest her soul. But what about my wishes? I tell you, Eldon, I pay you to protect *my* interests. Do you call this protecting my interests?" He tossed the document at the lawyer. "This will is dated just two weeks before my wife's death.

Find a way to use that in my favor. If Sheldon, Pfister, and Baker can't, I'll find someone who can."

"Yes, Mr. Parsons." Eldon rose with a sigh. "I'll be in touch." He exited the room.

"You'd better be," mumbled Andrew. "Higgins!"

His butler appeared at the door. "Sir?"

He motioned to the fireplace. "Another log."

"Yes, sir."

It was snowing again. Andrew could barely make out the tumbling flakes beyond the darkened window that threw his reflection back at him. The scowl which brought dread to the stoutest heart was distorted by the double-paned glass. He looked away, unable to meet his own gaze.

The doorbell rang. "What now!" he said. "Whoever it is, send them away."

He lifted his body, stiff and sore from rheumatism, out of his chair and stepped nearer to the fire. He rubbed his veined and wrinkled hands together, enjoying the warmth of the blaze. Above the mantle was another rendering, oddly enough by the same artist as the one in Tim's office. He traced the outline of the lodge with his fingers then slapped the top of the mantle. "No one is going to interfere with my plans. Do you hear me, nephew? No one!"

Higgins betrayed a look of surprise as he answered the bell. Eustace and Spencer stood before him in the opened doorway while snow fell all around them. It blew into the entryway making little puddles as it melted. "Mr. Parsons is seeing no one this evening," he said, and began to shut the door.

"Would you tell him it's about Heavenly Chalet."

"Heavenly what, sir?"

"Chalet. I think he'll want to see us."

The old man appeared in the doorway immediately after Higgins relayed the message. "What do you know about that?"

"May we come in?"

Andrew Parsons stood aside and motioned them in with his hand. Higgins shook his head as if to shake off his confusion, then went on about his business.

"Who told you about that?" Andrew repeated his demands. "Who are you?" His eyes narrowed suspiciously.

Eustace moved to the fire as if to warm himself. "'Heavenly Chalet,'" he read as he faced the rendering. "I noticed this the other day when we were here." He turned to the old man again.

"Then you must have eyes like a hawk," he replied, bristling with suspicion.

"Only when I remember to wear my glasses," he said, patting his shirt pocket. "When do you plan to build?"

"You know the answer to that as well as I," Andrew growled. "If my confounded nephew would take his nose out of my business I'd start tomorrow."

"It was your wife that put his nose there in the first place," Eustace countered.

"Leave my wife out of this," he snapped.

"It was her wish to see a church and a school built on that property," Spencer interjected, brushing snow-flakes from his coat.

"Blast your impudence!" cried the old man, turning on Spencer. "It was that son of my brother that forced

Helen into it, rest her soul. He's so . . . religious." The word fell off his tongue like poison.

"It helps in his profession," Eustace said.

"His profession. Is that what you call it? He hasn't earned an honest day's wages in his life. Sits back and waits for the collection plate to pass and takes what he likes of the money my employees work hard for. Serves them right, though, for giving it in the first place. And then he wants to deprive me of my right to free enterprise."

"Free enterprise? With the church's property?" Spencer asked.

"Who is this impudent creature?" He grimaced. "Hold your tongue or I'll thrash you!"

Spencer shot him an indignant look, but held his peace.

"Have you tried to talk to Tim about your side of this?" Eustace asked. "Have you offered some kind of compromise?"

"Compromise? Oh, certainly. He can build a church and I'll build a lift so his saints can go downhill fast!" Andrew roared at the humor of this, and even Eustace couldn't help but smile, though Spencer failed to see anything funny in it. "But why should I offer a compromise?" Andrew asked, returning to his previous temper.

"If you don't, you might lose altogether," Eustace replied. "The property was legally left to the church.

You're asking them to forfeit their dreams without offering anything in return. Is that fair?"

"We'll see what the courts have to say. I've got enough money to fight this all the way to the Supreme Court, and you can believe I will."

"But what a waste of time," Eustace said. The look on Andrew's face revealed that Eustace had hit a nerve. "You're not a young man anymore, Mr. Parsons. I understand this kind of suit could take years. Oh, well," he sighed, "it's your life." He made as if to go.

"What kind of compromise did you have in mind?" the old fox asked, skeptically.

"I didn't," Eustace replied, "but your nephew might."

Morning brought another crisp and clear day. The intense blue of the sky was in beautiful contrast to the new fallen snow. It was bitingly cold, but folks were out just the same. Some shopping, some working, but all talking about the canceled pageant. Misty and Raymond sat on the porch steps of the church, their chins cupped in their mittens. No smiles welcomed Eustace and Spencer as they approached.

Eustace joined the children on the steps. "My, don't we look unhappy today."

They raised their eyes to the visitors, but kept silent. Spencer picked up a pair of skates that rested beside Misty. "Why don't we go to the pond?"

"No, thanks," she replied, with an exaggerated sigh. Raymond echoed his sister's answer.

"Well, now," Eustace sat down beside the boy, "why are we so down in the mullygrubs?"

"In the what?" Raymond asked, crinkling his forehead.

"The mullygrubs," Eustace repeated. "That's where our joy goes if we don't hang on to it. I'd say your joy is definitely in the mullygrubs. And yours, too," he said to Misty. "What could have sent it there?"

Raymond shrugged his shoulders and dropped his chin back into his mittened hands.

"He doesn't get to be a shepherd," Misty answered glumly. "And I don't get to be an angel."

"No angel?" said Spencer sympathetically.

"Our Uncle Andrew won't let us have the Christmas pageant," Raymond explained. "I think it's because Christmas makes him sad. I think the pageant would make him like Christmas if he'd come to see it, only he won't."

"He might if he were asked," Eustace replied. "By the right person."

Raymond looked up at his friend, then lowered his eyes. "It doesn't matter since we're not having the pageant."

"What would you say if I told you that on Christmas Eve, Hometown will be having its pageant just like always, and that you'll be a shepherd, and you, my dear, will be an angel?"

"Really?" The children looked at one another, and then up at Eustace.

"Really?" echoed Spencer.

Eustace ignored the angel and addressed the children. "How big is your faith?"

Misty thought a moment, then said, "Mine's pretty big, but I don't know about Raymond's."

"Mine's pretty big, too," he said defensively.

"Well, that's good, because I think if your faith is big enough, we'll have the pageant. Will you believe?"

"I'll try," said Raymond.

"Me too," Misty promised.

"Look here, Spencer." Eustace studied the children's faces. "They've gotten their joy back from the mullygrubs. Do you see it?"

"I certainly do," he agreed, as smiles spread across their rosy faces. "That's much better."

"Raymond, do you want to go skating?" Misty asked.

"Sure," he said, and together they ran to the pond.

"Why on earth did you say that, Eustace?" Spencer asked when the children were gone.

"Say what, Spence?"

"That we're having the pageant."

"Aren't we?"

"Are we?"

"How big is *your* faith?"

"Really, Eustace, be serious. How do you plan to convince Mr. Parsons to let the church have the pageant?"

"I don't, actually. Tim's going to convince him."

"Tim? He's already been turned down once. You think he'll ask again?"

"He just might. Why don't we stop in and say hello. Since we're in the neighborhood."

They stood outside the door to Tim's office, but a familiar voice on the other side kept them from knocking.

"I tell you, Reverend, they're up to no good. I've seen it with my own eyes. I couldn't live with myself if I didn't warn you."

"I appreciate your warning, but I'm sure you're mistaken."

"Well, I'm going to keep my eye on them. I suggest you do the same."

The door opened and Emery Daniels stood face to face with Eustace and Spencer. He raised an eyebrow along with his hat, which he tipped to the angels. Then nodding to Tim, he stepped between them and left without another word.

"I hope we haven't come at a bad time," said Eustace.

"Not at all," Tim assured, but a look of dismay creased his brow.

"How's rehearsal coming along?" Eustace met Tim's look of surprise with an innocent smile.

"We've called off rehearsal, Eustace. I told you."

"I hate to see you give up without a fight. Maybe that's what your uncle wants, just to put up a good fight, and then concede."

"You don't know my uncle. He means to enforce the ordinance, and he has the law on his side. That pretty well settles it, Eustace."

"Maybe it does, but it couldn't hurt to continue with rehearsals. Just in case."

"And get everyone's hopes up? I couldn't do that."

Just then Beverly opened the door to Tim's office. "The phone," she said with a puzzled look, "it's for you."

"Just take a message, Bev. I'll call whoever it is later."

"I think you better take it," she said. "It's your uncle."

Startled, Tim picked up the phone on his desk. "Hello? Yes. Tonight?" He looked astonished as he hung up the receiver. "He wants to see me at his house at seven o'clock."

Seven

Caroline Perry arranged the centerpiece on the dining room table, ran the feather duster across the maple hutch, then gave a satisfied nod. Humming "O, Holy Night," she switched off the light and moved into the large entryway of her home. She dusted the arms and back of the settee, and touched the curtains decorating the window of the front door out of habit, for they seldom needed straightening. Everything was the picture of perfection. She moved toward the parlor, wondering why the doors were closed, then stopped when she heard voices filtering through the louvered slats.

"Have they gotten any mail, Walt?" she heard Emery ask.

"Not so much as a post card."

"What about calls, Oli? Has Clara put any through?"

"Not yet."

"Not even local calls? Say from Old Man Parsons?"

"No, but get a load of this," he remarked. "Old Man Parsons did make a call not an hour ago—to his nephew. Said he wanted to meet with him tonight at seven."

"No kidding," Emery said. "Wouldn't I like to be a fly on that wall tonight."

"What's going on in here?" Miss Perry frowned in the open doorway.

The gentlemen were startled, and looked from one to another not knowing what to say. Guilt spread over each face like a red mask. "Well?" she asked sternly.

Emery Daniels cleared his throat, but his voice still cracked when he answered. "We're just having a little meeting."

"Of what?" she demanded. "Busybodies Anonymous?" The gentlemen had never seen her so scolding, and averted their eyes from her gaze. "I can't believe my ears," she continued, "spying on our guests. Mr. Jeffries, you should be ashamed of yourself. And you, Mr. Bentley, taking advantage of Clara's position. Really, I don't know what to think."

"Don't you find them suspicious?" Emery ventured.

"Suspicious? Not in the least."

"You don't care who they are or where they came from?" he pressed.

"They're *gentlemen*," she replied, "that's all I care to know."

"Then you don't care to know that they've been hired by Andrew Parsons to bamboozle the Reverend out of his aunt's property?"

"What?" Her hand went to her mouth and her eyes grew large.

"That's my guess," Emery said.

"But why?"

"Everyone knows the old man has different ideas for that property. He can't get it out of his nephew, so he hired these fellas to use a little friendly persuasion. Don't you see?"

"They're sheep in wolves' clothing," Oliver assured. "I mean, well, you know."

"Oh, I just can't believe it. There must be another explanation."

"Well, believe what you want, Miss Perry," Emery concluded. "I'll believe the facts."

The gentlemen filed out of the parlor, leaving Miss Perry to sort out her thoughts. She dropped onto the sofa, a frown wrinkling her brow. "I can't believe it," she whispered again. "I refuse to believe it." But nagging thoughts assailed her just the same.

Dinner was a dreary affair that winter evening. The gentlemen, infected with Emery's suspicion, stole glances at Eustace and Spencer. More often than not they were caught in the act. Miss Perry tried in vain to spark a conversation, while Eustace, aware of the strain, remained nevertheless in his own thoughts. All cheerlessly went through the motions of eating, all except Dudley who loved Miss Perry's pot roast, and Spencer who loved everything.

"Dinner was delicious as always, Caroline," said Eustace, rising from the table, "but if you'll excuse us, we have business to attend to."

"Won't you have some chocolate cake?" she offered, though feebly.

The expression on Spencer's face was one of acceptance, but Eustace overrode it. "We couldn't just now. Maybe tonight when we come in."

She nodded, then began to clear the table.

Emery's eyes were on the two as they exited. He waited for Miss Perry to leave the dining room before he spoke. "They went upstairs to their room," he whispered. "I'll watch for them to go out, then follow them. I want to see where they go. My guess is they'll head straight for Old Man Parsons' house."

"What do you want us to do while you're gone, Emery?" asked Walter Jeffries. The others echoed the question.

"There's not much you can do, fellas. Just be on hand if I need you."

Eustace and Spencer went out just then. Once they were clear of the boarding house, Emery grabbed his coat and hat. With care and precaution he followed, keeping a safe distance behind, or so he thought.

They didn't go to Andrew's as expected, but went instead to his nephew's. "Uh-huh," Emery said under his breath, "keeping up the friendly pretense, I see."

Beverly let them in, and Tim stopped his pacing long enough to greet them. "Oh, am I glad you're here. I don't think I can go by myself."

"We'll go as far as your uncle's," Eustace said, "but this meeting is between the two of you."

"Do you think he's really going to let us have the pageant, Eustace? What could have changed his mind?"

"Whatever it's about, just don't let him get the upper hand," Eustace warned. "Be open-minded when necessary, but be equally firm."

"I wish you were going with me."

"I'll go with you," said Raymond, moving to his father's side.

"I don't know," he began hesitantly, but something changed his mind. "Maybe it *is* time you met your Uncle Andrew. Get your jacket, son."

Misty was not to be outdone. "Is it time I met my Uncle Andrew too?" she asked, her wide eyes looking up at Tim.

He smiled, then nodded his head. "Yes, Misty, I'd say it is. But both of you will have to be very quiet while Uncle Andrew and I discuss the pageant."

Raymond answered for both of them. "We promise."

Tim buttoned his coat, pulled on his hat and started for the door.

"Daddy?" Misty asked, lagging behind. "Shouldn't we pray first?"

Tim smiled as he answered, "Indeed we should. Would you like to lead?"

She nodded as they all took hands. "Dear God, please help us to be able to have the Christmas pageant so Raymond can be a shepherd and I can be an angel. And please help Uncle Andrew not to be so mean. Help my daddy not to be scared, and thank you for Eustace and Spencer. Amen."

"Amen," they said in harmony while Beverly wiped her eyes. She always wiped her eyes after Raymond and Misty prayed. She gave both of them a hug, accepted a kiss from Tim, and watched through the window until they were out of sight. "Dear God," she echoed in a whisper, "please help." She went into the kitchen to mix up a batch of Christmas cookies, but had she watched a moment longer, she'd have seen that Emery Daniels wasn't far behind Tim, the children, and their visiting angels.

They parted at the entrance to Andrew's estate. Eustace and Spencer watched as Higgins admitted Tim and his children.

"Now, Spencer," Eustace said, "it's my belief Tim could use our help, so we *will* be present at the meeting. They just won't know it."

"They won't know it? What on earth do you mean?"

"We're not going to let them see us," he explained.

"How will we get in without being seen, and where will we hide?"

Eustace whispered something to his friend, who in turn looked truly astonished.

"We can do that? How?"

"We simply choose to, Spencer," was the reply. "Follow me."

Emery hurried to where the angels had stood, stopping to peak around the corner of the entrance. There they were at the door.

"We'll have to create a diversion to draw Emery's attention from us," Eustace said. "He's behind that large tree over there."

"How do you always know?"

"It's just a feeling I get. Now, for that diversion."

Spencer heard the growl, low and threatening, before he ever saw the dog. Emery heard it, too, and by the time it rounded the house he was half way up a tree in Andrew Parsons' front yard. It looked as fierce as it sounded, and try as he might, Emery couldn't pacify the beast.

"That ought to keep his mind off of us for a while." Together they passed into the entry of Mr. Parsons' house.

They were all in the study when Eustace and Spencer went in. The latter was hesitant, to be sure, but when their entrance went unnoticed he relaxed a little. Andrew was sitting in a big leather chair behind his desk, frowning at Tim and trying not to notice the children.

"I'll come right to the point," he said, without a single pleasantry. "I must have that property, and I'm willing to make you an offer for it. That is if you're willing to be reasonable."

"The property?" Tim repeated. "Is that why you asked me to come?" He struggled to hide his disappointment.

"What else would we have to talk about?" the old man snapped.

"The pageant. I thought this was about the pageant."

"That was settled long before now," he growled. "Now, let's get down to business."

Tim was surprised, but he heard Eustace's voice reminding him once again, *whatever it's about . . . be open-minded, firm.* Okay, he was willing to listen and try, but before either one could say another word, Misty stepped forward to address her uncle.

"Why don't you like Christmas?" Her big blue eyes were fixed on the man. "Raymond says it's because it makes you sad."

"Raymond? Who's Raymond?" the old man grumbled. His eyebrows met in the middle of his forehead with a severe frown.

"He's my brother," she said, unaffected by Andrew's severity, "and he wants to be a shepherd. He has a lamb picked out at Mr. Wintzel's petting zoo, and my mommy has my wings nearly finished."

"Wings? What are you talking about, child?"

"For my angel costume."

Eustace and Spencer exchanged a smile and a wink, but Tim stepped forward, embarrassed. "I'm sorry, Uncle." He pulled Misty away. "Sit here and be quiet, sweetheart," he whispered, placing her on the sofa beside her brother.

Andrew made an audible grunt before turning his attention back to Tim. "Where were we? Oh, yes, the property."

Tim held up a hand to stop the old man. "Uncle Andrew, the church has no intention of giving up its claim to the property. If you insist on putting us through court then so be it, but we won't give up without a fight." Is that firm enough? he wondered, amazed at his boldness.

"Now, don't be so headstrong about this. I'm not asking you to give it up *exactly*." The old man searched for words. "I'm just asking you to be reasonable. You have a church. What do you need with another one? I'll tell you what. I'd be willing to pay off your mortgage. Then you could sell out, buy some property a little closer to town, and build to your heart's content." He sat back with a look of smug satisfaction at his generous offer.

"The church doesn't have a mortgage," Tim replied, "and the money we have is going toward a church and a school, not property."

Andrew looked stricken. "No mortgage? Why, that's un-American."

While he hunted for another approach, Eustace went to work on Tim. "That's a good point," he whispered in his ear. "Something a little closer to town would be far more practical."

"Can't he hear you?" Spencer asked, moving to the other side of Tim.

"It'll seem only as a thought; his own thought in fact."

"No kidding. That's remarkable. Will it work on him?" He pointed to Andrew.

"I don't know," Eustace replied. "He'd certainly be a challenge."

Spencer sauntered over and took a seat on the edge of his desk.

"I'll be honest, Uncle Andrew," Tim continued, "there's one drawback to Aunt Helen's property. It's eleven miles from town. I have to admit that's a very negative factor."

"Oh, *very*," Andrew agreed, softening his tone.

"But, we haven't any room to expand where we are." Eustace whispered another thought, and Tim spoke on. "What we need is another piece of property, in town, and large enough for our new facility. That parcel across from the pond would do nicely."

"Across from the pond? That's one of the choicest pieces of real estate left in Hometown. That's blackmail!" Andrew cried, "And you a reverend!"

"It's good business, Uncle. Surely you can understand that. We have something you want; you have something we want. I'm simply proposing a trade."

"Why there?"

"It's the perfect location for what the church wants to build. Fifteen acres isn't it? Just right for our new sanctuary and a school, with plenty of parking and room to grow. And I happen to know it was the church's first location choice when it was originally built. It wasn't available then, but it might be now."

"I plan to build—Well, never mind *what* I plan to build. I have a purpose for it and that's that."

"You have a purpose for all of your property, Uncle. You'll have to change some of your plans if we're to reach a compromise."

"I'd rather take a chance on losing the whole kit and caboodle than to give up that property." He set his jaw firmly. "No deal."

"Well, I guess we'll see you in court." He motioned to the children to get ready to leave, but his uncle's voice stopped him.

"Don't be in such a hurry," he said, holding up a hand. "What about the parcel on Pine Street, the one next to the bakery?"

"Too small."

"Well then, what about the one on Howard Avenue? It's twelve acres. We'll make it an even trade, and I'll even throw in the cost of the building permits."

"It's out of the way. No one would find us there."

"So much the better," he mumbled.

"It's the parcel across from the pond, or nothing." Tim stood facing his uncle, his arms folded across his chest, while the old man wrestled with the offer. When it appeared he wouldn't budge, Tim turned to go. "Like I said, we'll see you in court."

"Now, hold on a minute." The desire to see Heavenly Chalet built, running and raking in the cash overwhelmed him.

"Ask him to tell Tim *why* he wants to build Heavenly Chalet," Eustace said to Spencer. The young angel moved a little closer, then passed along his suggestion. Andrew's eyes registered the reception of the thought. His clenched fists registered the rejection of it.

"Go ahead," Spencer urged, "tell him. What can it hurt?"

Andrew picked up the portrait of his wife from off his desk. "Sixty years ago next month your Aunt Helen and I were married. We had our first and only major argument a week before the wedding. We fought about where to spend our honeymoon, of all things. She wanted to go to a resort up north and teach me to ski. I laughed at her. Said it wasn't dignified. We were going to the Bahamas and that was that. She gave in, and that's where we went." He placed the photograph back where it belonged, eased himself out of his chair, and walked over to the mantle. "Do you see this picture?" He indicated the rendering of Heavenly Chalet. Tim moved close enough to see the detail. "This was to be a gift to your Aunt Helen for our sixtieth wedding anniversary. A surprise. To make up for—" He stopped and cleared his throat. "I had it planned for months and months. Unfortunately, our anniversary was two weeks after her death. She never knew about Heavenly Chalet. And I never knew about her plans to donate the property to your church."

"I'm truly sorry, Uncle," Tim said. Eustace was right beside him before sentiment conquered reason. "But that doesn't change the fact that she *did* leave us the property."

"You're a stubborn young man," Andrew growled, shedding his softness.

"I come by it honestly."

Ignoring his comment, Andrew went on. "What will it take for you to give up your claim to Helen's property?"

"Another piece of property. The one across from the pond."

Andrew's eyes narrowed. "You drive a hard bargain, but I can see when I'm up against a wall. You sell the property your church is on now, and I'll give it to you for a good price."

Eustace nudged Tim. "No way," the nephew replied. "It'll be an even trade and you can consider it a steal. That parcel may be the best piece of real estate in Hometown, but it isn't half the land Aunt Helen's is. It'll be an even trade or no deal."

"Good boy," Eustace applauded.

"You really are stubborn," Andrew said, returning to his seat.

"It does make sense," Spencer whispered, but the old man turned away. "Think of the Chalet; it could be as good as done . . . for Helen."

Andrew faced Tim again, and with a look of pain he relented. "You're a tough negotiator, but it's a deal. I'll sign the property over to the church tomorrow."

"There's one other thing," Tim said, with Eustace at his side. "We want to have the pageant—in Town Square on Christmas Eve, just like always."

The children's eyes lit up as the old man's narrowed. "Nothing doing."

"But what could it hurt?" Spencer whispered.

"I won't do it!" he shouted.

"Look at the children," the young angel urged. "It would make them so happy."

They kept steady blue eyes on their uncle, the pleading in them unmistakable.

This was too much for an old man's heart, he thought. Sentimentality was getting the best of him. He squeezed his eyes closed to shut out the vision of theirs, and Tim's, and Helen's. It didn't help. He felt their gaze burning through his eyelids, and Helen's most of all. "I suppose your mother's gone to a lot of trouble with your wings?" he asked Misty. She nodded her head only slightly. "Well, we can't let them go to waste."

Tim hurried to the desk and shook his uncle's hand. "Thank you, Uncle." he said. "The whole town thanks you."

"I don't care about thanks. Just be here tomorrow and we'll seal it up with my lawyer."

"I'll be here," Tim assured him.

"Uncle Andrew," Misty moved around the desk to where he sat, "will you come to the pageant and see me?" Her eyes were wide and piercing, and hard to be denied.

"Me?" he mumbled. "Come to the pageant? Well, I—I don't know."

Raymond moved beside his sister. "Please," he asked. "Won't you come?"

"I'll have to check my calendar," he stammered. The color had drained from his face leaving it an ashen hue. "You'd better run along now. Higgins will show you out." He waved them away with a wrinkled old hand.

Eight

Eustace and Spencer didn't wait for the goodbyes. There was business to take care of just outside. Eustace, heard but not seen, whistled, and the growling under the tree stopped.

Emery heard the fading of the animal's paws as it retreated to places unknown. He scurried out of the tree as quickly as his frozen limbs would allow and turned the corner just as Tim and the children stepped out into the night. The angels took on their visible forms and stifled their laughter until Emery disappeared down the street, then had a great guffaw at the reporter's expense. In no time they were back at the church.

"Back so soon?" asked Eustace, meeting Tim and his children as they reached home.

"Eustace, it was great. You should have been there. Come in and I'll tell you all about it."

Beverly met them at the door and took coats and hats from everyone. "The coffee's ready," she said, "and cocoa." She hugged her children and received a kiss from each. "What did you think of your uncle?"

"He has a grumpy voice," Misty replied, "but he's only a little mean. I invited him to the pageant, Mama. Do you think he'll come?"

"The pageant?" she asked, turning to Tim.

"Wait until you hear." Together they relayed the evening's events.

"That was clever of you to hold out for the pageant," Spencer said, exchanging a furtive wink with Eustace.

"I tell you, Spencer, it was positively inspired." He beamed. "The whole evening was. Uncle Andrew tried to get the best of me, but I remembered your advice, Eustace, to be firm. I was and it worked."

"That's wonderful, Tim, but what about the church board?" Beverly asked. "Won't they have to vote on it?"

"Just as a formality. Tomorrow's Saturday. I'll call a special meeting in the morning and get it settled."

The clock over the mantle and Misty's drooping eyelids reminded Beverly it was past the children's bedtime. "I'll tuck them in and help them with their prayers," she said to Tim, who usually saw to this along with Beverly. It was a great opportunity to spend time with his children at the end of what were usually very busy days.

"Raymond?" Misty called to her brother when they were alone in their room.

"Hmm?" came a sleepy reply.

"Do you think he'll come? Uncle Andrew, I mean?"

"I don't know. Maybe. Go to sleep."

She lay in the darkness, closing her eyes tightly, but they wouldn't stay shut. "Raymond?" she said again. "Do you think he'll forget?"

"I don't think so." He turned in his bed and pulled the quilt up around his chin.

"Raymond?"

"Now what?"

"I hope he comes."

He turned toward his sister's bed and remembered the sad face of his uncle. "Me, too," he whispered, then the two children drifted off to sleep.

"I noticed something in your office yesterday," Eustace was saying to Tim. "A photograph; the one behind your desk."

Tim leaned back on the sofa. "It's a picture of the original building of our church when it was first dedicated. We've added on since then, as you can tell."

"And the gentleman in the photograph?"

"John W. Parsons, my granddad," he answered warmly.

"Tim's grandfather was the first pastor of that church," Beverly explained as she served the coffee.

"Really? Then he would be your uncle's—"

"Father," Tim finished.

Eustace pursed his lips and whistled. "The prodigal son who didn't leave town."

"Actually, he did. It all happened long before I was born, but I picked up enough bits and pieces of the story from my dad to put it all together. Granddad Parsons had two sons, my dad and Uncle Andrew. Like most fathers, he had hopes that one or both would follow in his footsteps. I think my dad would have, but he was sidetracked by the war. He ended up learning to fly, and became a commercial pilot after his discharge. That put the pressure on Uncle Andrew, but he had other plans." Tim plopped a spoonful of sugar into his coffee and took a sip. "Business was his interest. Granddad made the mistake of trying to pressure him into the ministry, and that's when he left. Went away to college and began to do quite well with investments and such. My granddad realized he'd been wrong in trying to fashion him into his own image, but he never got the chance to tell him. Year after year passed without a word from his son . . . until it was too late. He bought the mill and moved back to Hometown just after Granddad's funeral."

"So, we're dealing with guilt on top of grief," Eustace said. "A bad combination. But not a hopeless one." He held up a finger to emphasize the point.

"I don't know, Eustace," Tim confessed. "He certainly tests my faith."

Beverly sat at an upholstered chair, hand-stitching Misty's wings. "And mine," she added.

"But not theirs," Eustace said of the children, now fast asleep in their beds. "Maybe theirs will be enough."

Emery sat at his typewriter, but his thoughts weren't on the news. They were on the previous night's escapade. He knew he'd seen those fellas go into Andrew Parsons' house, but they sure hadn't been at the meeting with the Reverend. He knew that because he could see in through the study window from his tree-top perch. And they hadn't come out with Tim and his children, either. "The old man must have had them in hiding while he snared the prey," he muttered.

"Good morning, Emery," Tim called as he entered the reporter's office. "Beautiful morning, isn't it?"

"I guess if you're a penguin."

"It is pretty cold at that," he said, and shivered to prove it. "I have some business for you."

"Well, that's what I'm here for."

"I'd like you to run an announcement in the *Hometown Herald*. The pageant is back on," he said, to Emery's obvious amazement.

"You don't say! However did you manage that?"

"We're having a special board meeting in an hour. I'll tell you all about it then." He turned to go. "Oh, you'd better run that announcement all week. We want to be sure everyone sees it."

"Will do, Reverend. By the way, that's sure a mean dog your uncle has."

"Dog? Emery, my uncle doesn't have a dog."

The board members arrived promptly at ten. There were six altogether, and that included Emery, Oliver, and Dudley. The pastor, who conducted the meetings, was the seventh member, but he couldn't vote unless it was to break a tie. Beverly brought in a tray loaded with refreshments, then left them to their business. Eustace and Spencer came in as well . . . but no one was aware.

"Thank you all for coming on such short notice," Tim began. "I have some business I think you'll all find exciting."

"Did the Ladies Aid Committee decide on the new choir robes?"

"Not yet, Dudley. We'll have to keep them in prayer a little longer. Speaking of prayer, let's begin." They all bowed their heads for Tim's invocation. He allowed them a minute to pour a cup of coffee, and then began. "Yesterday, I received a call from my uncle. He said he wanted to see me." Oliver looked at Dudley, and recalled the sting of Miss Perry's indignation. "I knew it must be about church business, but it wasn't quite what I expected. Eustace and I were speaking about the pageant when my uncle called, so I naturally associated the call with that."

"You seem to spend a lot of time with those fellas," Emery interrupted.

"Yes, I guess I do. Anyway, when I got to my uncle's last night he didn't want to see me about the pageant at all, but rather about my Aunt Helen's property."

Emery was immediately suspicious, which caused Oliver and Dudley to be suspicious as well. "Has he decided not to contest?" asked the reporter.

"Not exactly," Tim replied, wishing he'd stop interrupting. "We have."

"What?" The board members exchanged surprised looks and began murmuring amongst themselves.

"Let me explain." Tim waited a moment for the tumult to subside. "We've all talked about the disadvantage of that property being so far out of town."

"That may be true, but that's no reason to give it up, Reverend."

"We haven't given it up, Emery, not exactly. We've made a trade. At least, if we so decide here today."

Emery's eyes narrowed. "What kind of a trade?"

"You know the lot north of Town Square, the one across from the skating pond? It's ours if we want it. My uncle is willing to make an even exchange."

"Why wouldn't he?" Emery said with a sneer. "That lot isn't half the property your aunt left the church."

"True. But it's far more suited to our needs."

"I think the pastor has a good point there," said Jonathan Parks, another member of the board. "The value of it lies in the necessity, not the dollar figure. I think we ought to hear him out."

"I think he's been taken in by those two strangers if you want to know the truth," Emery replied. "That's why they came here in the first place. To lull you, Reverend, along with the rest of us, into thinking we've been made a good offer. Well, I'm not buying it. I've said all along they're in cahoots with your uncle, and now I'm certain of it."

Eustace and Spencer were surprised at this bit of information. So was Tim. "What do you mean, 'in cahoots,' Emery? They don't even know my uncle."

"Oh, don't they? I've seen them go into his house with my own eyes twice. The first time, the very day after they came to town, no doubt to get instructions. The second time, last night."

"Last night?" Tim repeated. "They couldn't have."

"They could and they did," Emery said.

"But how would you know? Where were you?"

Emery shifted in his folding chair. "Never mind how I know, I just know. It's my business to be aware of what goes on in Hometown. Now what do you have to say about those fellas?"

"I say we don't worry about them, and get down to the business we came here for," Jonathan said, pushing his glasses up on his nose.

"But I say they've a whole lot to do with that business," Emery returned, slamming his hand on the table.

"Now, gentlemen, let's keep our heads," Tim said, "and let's keep to the business at hand. Jonathan's right; Eustace and Spencer aren't concerned in this matter."

"I don't know, Pastor." Oliver paused, as if reluctant to go on. "I'm afraid I have to agree with Emery. I think they're all mixed up in this."

Tim looked perplexed. "What do the rest of you say? Are you of the same opinion? Do you feel there's been collusion on the part of these gentlemen and my uncle to cheat the church out of my aunt's property?"

"Now hold on, Reverend." Emery held up a hand. "Collusion is a strong word. That isn't what I said."

"It's what you implied."

"I only mean to present the facts. You draw your own conclusions. It just seems a little fishy to me, that's all."

Tim sighed. "We're getting nowhere. We haven't once kept to the purpose of our meeting."

"The Reverend's right," Jonathan said. "We're just wasting time. I promised the kids we'd go cut a tree. Now, can we get on with this?"

Eustace moved to Emery's chair and put a hand on his shoulder. "Everyone's getting impatient," he whispered. "Even your buddies are beginning to question." Emery looked at Dudley and Oliver, who were responding to Spencer's promptings with expressions of doubt.

"Let me ask you this," Tim said to Emery. "Do you think my aunt's property is a good place for us to build our church and school?"

"Well, we've all made mention that it *is* a little far from town."

"Yes, we have. Now, do you think the property across from the pond is a good place to build our church and school?"

"It might be."

"Emery!" Jonathan cried. "Is it or isn't it, for Heaven's sake?"

"It might be," he repeated, "if we were to be compensated for the difference in value."

"You mean with money?" Tim shook his head. "My uncle would never go for it. He already thinks he's done more than his part."

"Besides," Jonathan added, "property in town is worth more per acre than property outside of town."

"That's a good point, Jonathan," Tim declared.

Eustace gave Spencer a wink. "Good thinking, Spence."

"If you take that into consideration, both properties are probably of equal value." Jonathan looked at his watch. "Now, can we please vote?"

"Just a minute," Emery said.

"What is it now?"

Tim held up a pacifying hand. "It's all right, Jonathan. We need to look at it from all sides. If Emery still has a question, we need to discuss it. Emery, do you have a question?"

All eyes were on him as he tried to think of one. It just seemed fishy to him. And those two fellas especially seemed fishy.

"But how do you put that into words?" Eustace whispered. "Words that would convince *them*, and keep *you* from looking bad?"

"Well," Jonathan broke the silence.

"It's just that—"

"Emery!"

"Oh, all right. I guess not," Emery said with a pout.

"Then let's vote."

"Okay," Tim said. "All those in favor of trading the properties, raise your hand." Jonathan's hand went up immediately, as did those of the two members who sat on either side of him. Oliver and Dudley both looked at Emery, then slowly, very slowly, they each raised a hand.

"Okay," Emery growled, and put his hand up too. He knew when he was beaten.

Tim let out a sigh of relief. "There's one other thing," he said as the others scooted their chairs out to leave. "My uncle has also agreed to allow the pageant to be held in Town Square. We're on for Christmas Eve."

Smiles and congratulations came from the board members, all except Emery, who continued to pout. When they left, Tim gave out another sigh of relief. By one-thirty, the papers were signed, and by three o'clock, rehearsals were underway.

Rehearsals were a frantic affair with Christmas Eve just a week off. Tim worked with the choir, while Bev directed the drama. Everyone worked on the props, including Eustace and Spencer.

It was awfully cold that December, everyone said so, and poor Spencer just couldn't adapt. "You don't suppose it was like this when Jesus was born, do you?" he asked, wrapping a muffler around his neck. He remained in a constant shiver, and had to set his jaw to keep his teeth from chattering.

"No, I don't think so, Spence, but He was born in Bethlehem, not Hometown, you know."

"Is it very different?"

"Quite. I doubt Bethlehem has seen a flake of snow from that day to this."

"It sounds like an inviting place." He looked out a window at the white mounds. "It's nice to look at, but it's so unpleasant in every other respect."

"Many folks would disagree. Really, they would. Look at the children. They enjoy it immensely. If Heavenly Chalet were completed, you'd see just how recreational winter can be."

"Amazing."

"What's the matter, Spence? Getting a little homesick?"

"A lot homesick, actually. I can hardly remember what it's like to be warm."

"I expect you'll find out before long."

"Do you think so?"

Eustace nodded. "Yes, I do."

"I've given the choir a twenty minute break," said Tim, joining his friends. "Thought I'd come see how the stable's progressing."

"If it looks half as good as the choir sounds I'd say we're doing well."

"Thanks, Spencer. Wow! It's amazing what can be done with a little cardboard and paint. You two have a talent for this. It's the most authentic stable we've ever had."

"It was Eustace's design," Spencer said.

"I just made a few little changes on the old one. If you don't mind, I'd like to make an adjustment or two on the manger. It looks more like a cradle on legs than a feeding trough."

"Be my guest," Tim said. "You're doing a great job." He left them to check on costumes.

"What's a feeding troth?" Misty asked.

"I thought you were outside throwing snowballs at your brother," Eustace said. He hadn't seen her come in with Tim.

"I was, but he threw some back and I got cold."

"Oh." Spencer knelt down beside her. "I can certainly sympathize."

She took off her wet mittens, blew into her hands, then rubbed them together. "What's a feeding troth?" she asked again.

"It's a feeding *trough*," Eustace corrected, "and it's a wooden box where hay and other feed was placed for the animals in the stable. Joseph and Mary used the trough as a bed for baby Jesus."

"Mama said they put baby Jesus in a manger."

"And your mama's right. Manger is another word for feeding trough. It just sounds a little nicer."

"Why did they put baby Jesus in there and not in a cradle? I had a cradle and so did Raymond. Mama lets me use it for my dolls now."

"I'm afraid they didn't have a cradle."

"But Joseph was a carpenter. Why didn't he make one?"

"Well now, Misty, that's a very good question. I think Joseph probably did make a cradle for baby Jesus, but they had traveled a long way from where they lived in Nazareth to Bethlehem where Jesus was born."

"I've heard of Nazareth," she said.

"They couldn't carry much on that trip, certainly nothing as big as a cradle, and I think they both were hoping they'd get back home before the baby was born. But it had to happen just the way it did, for a prophet—do you know what a prophet is?" When Misty nodded Eustace continued. "For a prophet named Micah had foretold that baby Jesus would be born in Bethlehem long before it happened."

"How did he know?"

"God told him."

"God knows everything, doesn't He?"

"He certainly does."

"Then why didn't He put a cradle in the stable so that baby Jesus would have a bed?"

Spencer and Misty both looked to Eustace for an answer, but he was obviously stumped. "Well, now. I'll have to work on that one," he said, and returned to the task at hand.

Miss Perry placed the last bulb on the tree as Eustace and Spencer came in. "How does it look?" She looked pleased as could be with her handiwork.

"Wonderfully festive," they both agreed.

"And the smell," she said, filling her nostrils with the scent of pine, "there's nothing quite so fresh. Let's see how it looks from outside." She switched off the parlor lights as they went out. Through the large front window the tree shimmered as tinsel caught the colors of the twinkling lights woven through the ornamented branches. "It's the prettiest ever . . . but I say that every year."

"Something smells delicious," Spencer said, hanging his coat on the rack.

"It's wassail. My favorite. I'll get us all a cup." She went into the kitchen, then soon returned with a tray of steaming mugs.

"Wassail, you say?" Spencer inhaled its spicy fragrance, then took a sip of the hot cider. "Mmm, it's very good."

She nodded. "If you don't mind my saying so, you both seem so unaccustomed to our ways, almost like foreigners. Are you really from anywhere around here?"

"Our home is rather distant in the physical sense," Eustace admitted, "but it's nearer than you might imagine."

"At least to some," Spencer added.

"For beauty it's unsurpassed. There's no place I'd rather live. It's simply out of this world."

"You make it sound like paradise."

"It has been called by that name."

"I guess we're all partial to the places we live." She shrugged. "Why else would we live there? I've spent my whole life in Hometown, and like you, Eustace, there's no place I'd rather live this side of Heaven. We have so much to offer in Hometown—friendly people, four distinct and lovely seasons, and before long it appears we'll have our very own ski lodge. Can you imagine?" She eyed Eustace as she took a sip of the wassail. "I try to make my boarders feel right at home," she went on. "My goodness, we're like one big, happy family. I do hate to have any of my rooms vacant. It makes the house seem too empty. Of course, there's never a problem finding new boarders, we're in such a desirable location. But we get used to having certain faces around. I've gotten used to yours already."

"Our stay here has been delightful, Caroline. We couldn't ask for better accommodations," Eustace said.

"I'm glad you think so. It means a great deal to me."

"I must tell you, however, that Spencer and I won't be staying on much longer. Our business here is nearly finished."

"Yes, I was afraid of that." She shook her head. "Paradise awaits?"

"For all of us, Caroline. For all of us."

"But you'll be here for the pageant, won't you?"

"We wouldn't miss it," he assured her, "not for the world."

"Well, if you'll excuse me, I have some baking to do. Don't you just love the smells of Christmas?"

Spencer waited for the door of the kitchen to swing shut. "I think she's going to miss you."

A smile touched Eustace's lips. "We've met some wonderful people, haven't we?"

"Yes, we have. And some not-so-wonderful."

"Speaking of Andrew Parsons, I have some business to attend to." He reached for his coat and scarf. "I won't be long."

"Don't you want me to go?" Spencer asked, but Eustace could tell his heart wasn't in it.

"Not this time," he said. "Stay and enjoy the fire."

His eyes reflected the warm glow of the blaze and he smiled. "You won't have to ask me twice."

Eustace found what he wanted on the bookshelf in Tim's office, then headed to Andrew's home. He passed a few evening pedestrians as they hurried home from shopping, but they weren't aware of him. Neither was Higgins as he passed him in the hallway. He entered the study. No one was present. "Good," he said as he went about his business, then he left, leaving the room *almost* as he had found it.

Emery heard him go up to his room at Miss Perry's boarding house where Spencer had already retired for the night. As usual he tried to listen through the wall that separated his room from theirs. Every night he heard their muffled conversation, and strained to catch a word or two, but thick walls and Dudley's snoring filtering in from across the hall, kept him from distinguishing one word from another. He'd read in detective novels that you could place a glass against a wall and listen that way, but he never could remember to bring one up with him when he retired at night. He looked around for something he might use instead. There was nothing.

He lay down on his bed, and when he did, his eye lit on the vent at the top of the wall. He liked his bedroom cold, even in the dead of winter, so his side of the vent was closed. But maybe . . . The young one was always shivering . . . He moved a chair without a sound and placed it beneath the vent. He stepped up onto it, then quietly slid the handle until the vent was open. His hunch was correct; their vent was open too.

". . . get our promotion," he heard Spencer say. "I think we've done a good job."

"We're not finished yet."

"A few more days and we will be. I can't wait to see the Chairman sign our promotion."

"Don't be hasty, Spence. There's more to this job than a switching of properties. We didn't come all this way just for that."

"Between that and the pageant, we've made everyone happy, and if Andrew Parsons is happy, we've done our work."

"I knew it," Emery whispered. "Old Man Parsons is signing their paychecks, sure as the world. I wonder why they call him 'Chairman.' There must be a whole lot more to this than meets the eye."

He listened to the silence that followed until his curiosity got the best of him. Standing on his tip toes he looked through the vent . . . right into a pair of emerald eyes.

"'Evening," said Eustace, startling Emery severely.

"I—I—was just opening my vent."

"Well now, I was just closing mine. Goodnight."

Emery stepped down off the chair and pushed it back into place. "You'd think he knew I was there," he said, mad and embarrassed all at the same time. "But, I heard enough to know I'm on the right track. You can fool all the others," he said, "but you're not fooling me. I intend to find out what's going on, and when I do I'll expose the whole lot of you."

Nine

The weather was cold but clear the day before Christmas Eve. The forecast promised more of the same.

"We may not have *the* star, but at least it won't be cloudy," Tim said, as the choir and drama characters gathered in Town Square for dress rehearsal.

"I don't think it would matter if it was. Everyone's just excited that we're having the pageant." Beverly smiled at her husband. "You make a handsome Joseph. Why don't you get the choir situated? I'll need you in a few minutes."

Beverly took her place on the stage, knelt in the ethereal beam of the spotlight for the opening scene, and waited for the angel Gabriel to appear unto Mary. The beginning notes of his song rang out, but Gabriel was nowhere to be seen.

"Stop the music!" Tim called from his director's platform. "Gabriel! Where's Gabriel? Oh, there you are." He looked relieved to see Mike Featherston step through the crowd of cast and crew members. "Take your place and we'll start over."

Mike shook his head and handed Tim a note.

He read the note, then read it again. "Laryngitis! Mike, you can't do this to me." He covered his face and rubbed his aching forehead, then remembered this wasn't just about him. "Oh, hey, Mike, I'm sorry. What am I saying?" He placed a hand on his shoulder and said a prayer for him. "Go on home and take care of yourself. And don't forget to gargle."

Beverly stepped down from the stage and joined her husband. "Tim, this has never happened before. What are we going to do?"

"I don't know, honey."

"Could you sing Gabriel's part if we find another Joseph?"

"I'm not a tenor," he said. A frown creased his brow and he began to pace. Suddenly, he snapped his fingers. "But, I know someone who is!" He ran across the road to Miss Perry's boarding house and rapped at the door.

"Why, Pastor Tim! What a nice surprise," Miss Perry said, wiping her hands on her apron. "How is rehearsal going?"

"We've run into a problem, Miss Perry. Is Spencer here by any chance?"

"I believe so. Please, come in."

Tim waited anxiously as Miss Perry went to fetch him, and smiled broadly when Spencer came into view. "Spencer! Wow, am I glad you're here. I need your help. Gabriel has laryngitis and there's no one who can do his song but you."

"Me?"

"Yes, you. I know you know his song, and there's no one who could sing it like you. Please say you'll do it."

"I know his song," Spencer agreed, "but what about his lines?"

"They're straight out of the Gospel of Luke. Are you familiar with Luke?"

Spencer smiled and nodded. "I should say so."

"Then please say you'll do it?"

"Okay then, I will." He hurried out with Tim, with Eustace right behind them.

Rehearsal ended without another catch and had gone as well as dress rehearsals can go. The star in the East needed one more coat of glitter, but the wise men arrived just the same. And a shepherd or two forgot to be sore afraid when the heavenly host appeared, but these were minor details.

Eustace and Spencer were invited home with the Parsons for dinner that afternoon. It was their first experience with Chinese take-out. "Spencer you're a godsend," Beverly declared as she served the chow mein. "You were made for the part. I got goose bumps all over when you delivered your lines. 'Hail, thou that art highly favored, the Lord is with thee.' It wasn't so much what you said, but how you said it. I could imagine how it must have been when Gabriel appeared to Mary."

"She's right. You were outstanding." Tim patted his shoulder. "I can't thank you enough for filling in."

"I'm only too happy to oblige, but I do have one question. What on earth is laryngitis?"

Everyone laughed at Spencer's great joke—everyone but Eustace. He only shook his head.

Andrew Parsons paced the length of his study, stopping every now and then before the mantle. It was the day before Christmas and there, under the rendering of Heavenly Chalet, stood the only indication in his house that it was: a lone Christmas card offering Season's Greetings. Of course, it was from Tim and his family. Who else would think about him now that Helen was gone? He didn't mind the card, though it was a bit too sentimental for his tastes, but why had they let the child add that silly postscript? Couldn't they just sign it and be done with it? He opened the card and read it again. *Dear Uncle Andrew, I hope you*

have a Merry Christmas and please come to see Raymond and me in the pagent. Love Misty. Why, the child couldn't even spell the word correctly.

Higgins brought in his dinner tray and set it near the fire. He waited for Mr. Parsons to take his seat, then moved it in place. He unfolded the napkin and placed it across his lap. "Would you care for coffee with your supper, sir?" Andrew made an affirmative grunt, and Higgins poured from the silver service. "Would there by anything else, sir?" He waved him away, and Higgins withdrew.

The food was no doubt as good as it always was, and as appetizing as dinner for one can be, but Andrew had no appetite. He moved the tray away and sat back in his chair. When he did, something jabbed him in the side. A book no doubt had slid between the arm of the chair and the cushion. Yes, that was it, a book. He placed it on the table beside him, but even before his hand let go of it, he realized it wasn't the book he'd been reading. It was an old book, worn and faded. It was . . . yes, a Bible.

"How did that get there?" he muttered, but he picked it up again to examine it. Initials, quite faint now from years of handling, were engraved on the bottom of the front cover. He held it under the lamp's light and adjusted his trifocals to make them out. J.W.P.

With a stirring in his heart, he ran his hand over the cracked leather and slowly opened the front cover. There, in a longhand script he well recalled, was the inscription: *"To my beloved husband, John, at his ordination."* It was signed by Andrew's mother. He closed his eyes and envisioned the face of the woman he'd not seen in so many years. He even thought he caught a whiff of the scented powder she always wore, and then it was gone. How had his father's Bible gotten here? He hadn't seen it in years. Where had it come from?

A ribbon, faded and frayed, extended out of the bottom. He opened it to the page it marked, perhaps the last page his father had read. His eyes fell to a passage that was underlined and he spoke the words out loud. *"And she brought forth her firstborn son, and wrapped him in swaddling clothes, and laid him in a manger; because there was no room for them in the inn."*

He studied the fire through eyes unwontedly blurred, his mind conjuring up a lifetime of forgotten memories, and all the while his eye was drawn to the card on the mantle. It wasn't the carolers in their wintry garb singing the blessings of Christmas that attracted him, nor the wreath on the door that stood open before them. The snow-laden trees in the background didn't vie for his attention. All in all it made a quaint little scene, but what did he care for quaint little scenes? No, it was nothing on the front that drew him to it. It was that silly postscript inside. *Please come and see me . . .*

What was it about children that allowed them to wiggle their way into a person's thoughts uninvited? Was it their innocence, their candor? Yes, that and those trusting blue eyes that could melt the ice from around the coldest heart. Even a heart like Andrew Parsons'.

He closed his eyes against the intruding thoughts, but there before him in vivid color was the boy he used to be. A boy holding a shepherd's staff, kneeling before a manger, in Hometown's very first Christmas pageant. He stood beside an exuberant Joseph, played by his father, in the production he'd always dreamed about.

"Higgins!" he called, as the vision faded away.

The butler left his simple dinner to see to his employer. "Is something wrong, sir?"

"No, confound it!"

"Your supper is untouched, sir. Would you prefer something else? I could ask Cook—"

"Get my coat," he snapped, "then bring the car around. We're going out."

"Out, sir?"

"Yes, out!"

"But, your rheumatism, sir."

"Confound my rheumatism! We're going out!"

"Very good, sir."

Eustace adjusted his costume as he and Raymond waited back stage for their cues. "Are you nervous?" he asked the boy.

Raymond nodded. "I'm just glad I don't have to say anything. Do you think Spencer's nervous? He has to sing."

"Oh, maybe a little."

"Have you ever been in a pageant, Eustace?"

"Well, sort of. A long time ago."

"When you were a little boy?"

"In a manner of speaking. It was Christmas and we were preparing for this same event."

"Were you a shepherd like me?"

"No, Raymond, I wasn't a shepherd. I was an angel."

"Were you scared?"

"More than anything I was overwhelmed."

Just then, Tim came hurrying back. "Eustace! You're not going to believe this! It's another case of laryngitis. My angels are dropping right and left!"

"Who is it now?"

"Oliver Bentley! The Angel of the Lord!"

"Oh, dear, you can't have a pageant without the Angel of the Lord."

"Isn't that the part you played?" Raymond asked.

"You've played the part?" Tim's face was covered in relief. "That's great."

"Well, actually, I had a supporting role."

"No matter," he said with a wave of his hand. "Do you remember the lines?"

"Oh, yes, I remember them. Word for word."

"Then you'd better get into costume. The pageant begins in five minutes."

Eustace had no chance to refuse, for Tim was off again.

"Five minutes?" Raymond said, then hurried away to find his place with the other shepherds.

"What are you doing here, Spence? You're about to go on."

"You were with the Angel of the Lord when he made the proclamation to the shepherds in Bethlehem?" Spencer couldn't have been more surprised.

"I was. And it appears that I'm about to be promoted. Temporarily, of course. Now, you'd better get in position, and I'd better get in costume."

There was a reverent silence in Town Square as the pageant got underway. Everyone in Hometown was present. Absolutely *everyone*.

Higgins studied Andrew Parsons through the rearview mirror. "Are you certain you don't want to get out, sir? You could see and hear a little better."

"I'm certain," he growled, but his voice was less menacing than usual. He stretched his neck to see through the branches of the pine tree that hid their car. Town Square was filled with people, happy people, waiting excitedly for the pageant to begin. Somewhere in the pit of his stomach there was a churning. Not the kind that his stocks and bonds often caused, but a different kind, more of a nervous anticipation.

From the depths of his memory he knew he'd felt this before. But when? Then seeing Raymond amongst the assembling shepherds he knew. It was a night like this, eons ago. The faces of the crowd were different, but the anticipation was the same.

"Let down the window, just a bit," he said to Higgins. "I like my fresh air, you know." He wrapped a woolen blanket closely about him and shivered as the narrator stepped to the microphone and began to read:

"And in the sixth month the angel Gabriel was sent from God unto a city of Galilee, named Nazareth, to a virgin espoused to a man whose name was Joseph, of the house of David: and the virgin's name was Mary."

Beverly and Spencer played their parts well, and the audience loved Spencer's song. The richness of his voice filled the night with a heavenly sound to be sure. Mary and Joseph found their way to the stable, and there in the darkness the baby Jesus was born.

Off in the distance the shepherds were keeping watch over their flocks by night. One in particular tended a real live lamb.

"And, lo, the Angel of the Lord came upon them," read the narrator, "and the glory of the Lord shone round about them: and they were sore afraid."

"Fear not," said Eustace, delivering his lines, "for behold I bring you good tidings of great joy, which shall be to all people. For unto you is born this day in the City of David a Savior, which is Christ the Lord, and ye shall find the babe wrapped in swaddling clothes, lying in a manger."

"And suddenly there was with the angel a multitude of the heavenly host praising God," the narrator said as the choir broke into song. Hearts filled with joy at the beauty of the music. "Glory to God in the highest," they sang, "and on Earth peace, good will toward men." Angels of all sizes, besides those in the choir, lined the steps of City Hall. Andrew searched the angelic lineup until he found the one he was looking for. There she was, the little one, proudly wearing her wings. She was scanning the rows of spectators hopefully, and he knew with a twinge she was looking for him.

The shepherds hurried to the stable and found baby Jesus lying in a manger just like Eustace had said. Then they glorified and praised God for all the things they had heard and seen. The wise men came next, following the star. Placing their treasures before the manger, they fell down and worshiped the Babe.

The living nativity was complete and all eyes were on the stable as the choir continued to sing. The atmosphere was alive with worship, and when the choir broke into "The Hallelujah Chorus" for the finale, there wasn't a dry eye in Town Square. It was glorious. Even Eustace thought so, and he, of all present, should know.

Ten

Christmas morning brought a light snowfall, which continued throughout the day. Eustace and Spencer had breakfast with Caroline, who was then going to her sister's in Elmwood.

"Are you sure you won't come along? Esther would love to have you."

"We promised Tim and Beverly we'd have dinner with them," Eustace replied. "But we thank you and your sister for the invitation."

"Well, if I know Beverly she'll send you home more stuffed than the turkey, but I have a pecan pie in the refrigerator. You're to help yourselves."

"You shouldn't have gone to the trouble."

"It's not a bit of trouble. Besides, it's the least I could do considering I have a pair of angels in the house."

She smiled at Eustace and Spencer, whose breath had caught in their throats. "You were both magnificent last night." They exhaled, understanding her meaning, and returned her smile. "Who would have thought you'd end up in the pageant, and both of you angels?"

"Who, indeed?"

"But you've done that kind of thing before, I could tell. You were so natural, and so authentic. Merry Christmas, Mr. Daniels."

"Same to you," he said, entering the dining room.

"I was just saying what a wonderful job these gentlemen did in the pageant last night. Don't you agree?"

"Not bad."

The mantle clock in the parlor chimed the hour of ten. "Oh, dear, it's time I got ready," she said. "Esther's expecting me in an hour."

They stood as she left the room, then sat back down in an awkward silence. "I understand you'll be leaving soon," Emery said at length.

"Yes, our business here is finished."

"And you'll be going back to—What was the name of that place?"

"We call it home."

"How clever. I gather the *Chairman* is pleased with your work?"

Eustace ignored a startled look from Spencer. "The Chairman?"

"He had you come down here, didn't he? That *is* who you work for?"

"You're very sharp, Mr. Daniels. It's hard to get anything past you."

Emery sat back with an air of satisfaction. "It's my business to read between the lines."

"Please read on."

"I don't understand why Old Man Parsons didn't propose trading property on his own. I guess he needed you fellas to make the Reverend think it was his idea. That was clever of him. He got what he wanted and it saved him a costly court battle."

"And a great deal of time," Eustace added.

"That, too. I guess when you get right down to the bottom of it there was no harm done. It's lucky for you two there wasn't, because I've been onto you since you got here. I was about to expose you, but since you seem so cooperative I'll make you a deal. You pack up and leave Hometown for good and I'll keep this business under my hat . . . since no harm was done."

"That's big of you."

"You can call it my Christmas present to you."

"I guess we have no choice but to comply, right, Spence?"

"Right."

"Smart choice," he said, rising to go. "I do have one question, though. What's he the Chairman of?"

Eustace motioned for Emery to move closer, then said in a whisper, "We call it The Committee, but keep that under your hat, too . . . since no harm was done. Merry Christmas, Emery."

The turkey was nearly finished when Eustace and Spencer arrived at the Parsons' that Christmas afternoon. The smells that greeted them were out of this world, and they said so. After enthusiastically receiving the new sled Eustace and Spencer brought the children, Raymond hurried them into the living room to show off his Christmas gifts. Eustace said the sled dropped out of the sky, but of course, no one believed it.

"And we have something for you," Raymond said proudly. Eustace and Spencer unwrapped festive packages and found new mufflers and gloves inside. "They're from Misty and me."

"Just what I always wanted." Spencer beamed as he hung the scarf around his neck. "Thank you both, very much."

"You're welcome," replied the boy. But Misty sat silent on the couch, her eyes cast downward. "She's been like that all day," her brother whispered.

"What on earth for?" Spencer whispered back.

"Because he didn't come."

"Who didn't come?"

"Uncle Andrew. He didn't come to the pageant."

"Well, don't feel too bad, Misty. You tried, and that's very important. Isn't it important, Eustace?"

"Oh, very," he said, then sat down beside her. "And I'll tell you a secret, Misty. He was closer to coming than you think."

She looked up at him with a question in her eyes. "Really?"

"Really. And all because of you."

"Me?"

Eustace smiled and nodded. "Do you know what a miracle is?"

"I know what it is, but it's hard to explain."

Eustace smiled again. "That's what makes it a miracle. And it happens because someone believes it will. Maybe it doesn't come all at once, but that doesn't matter, so long as it comes. Does that make sense?"

"I think so," she said, her voice faltering. "But I wanted him to see my wings."

"They were the nicest wings I ever saw," Spencer said.

"I think so, too," Eustace agreed. "Besides, there's always next year. A lot can happen in a year."

As she hugged her friend, a smile pulled at the corner of her mouth. Not enough to make her dimple show, but it was a start.

"Dinner's served!" Tim called, and everyone took their places around the table. They all joined hands as Tim prepared to offer a special holiday blessing.

"Daddy?" Misty said. "Will you pray that Uncle Andrew won't be lonely today, and that he'll be with us next year?"

"Now that will take *some* miracle," he said, "but we can pray."

Misty smiled, showing both dimples this time, while Eustace and Spencer exchanged a wink.

The feasting began.

Spencer enjoyed himself tremendously as he tried new and luscious delectables. He ate with an unquenchable appetite, it seemed, much to the delight of his hostess. Every morsel was savored and lavished with praise.

The pie was eaten and the day well spent. Eustace and Spencer had enjoyed their Christmas with the Parsons, but now it was time to leave.

"Will you go skating with us tomorrow?" Raymond asked as Eustace put on his coat.

"Tomorrow we leave for home," Eustace replied, to everyone's disappointment.

"So soon?" Beverly asked. "We hate to see you go."

"We really must, I'm afraid."

"Will we see you again?" Tim asked.

"Oh, yes. I'm certain of it." With an abundance of hugs and handshakes they were off.

They were already through the gate when they heard Misty's voice calling them to stop. Breathlessly, she caught up with them and presented Spencer with yet another gift—her wings from the pageant.

"Misty, I'll treasure these forever." He bent down to receive a kiss on the cheek, his very first.

Taking leave of Miss Perry the following morning was no less difficult. She tried to persuade them to change their minds, but to no avail.

"You haven't even had your breakfast," she said. "How far will you get on empty stomachs?"

"We'll be fine," Eustace assured, ignoring a look from Spencer to the contrary. With words of thanks they started on their way.

"I do hope I'll see you again," she called, but even before she spoke the words she felt an assurance that she would.

"This has been quite an adventure," Spencer commented as they neared the edge of town. "I'll never forget it. Who would have thought people could come to mean so much to an angel? Even people like Emery Daniels and Andrew Parsons."

"It's impossible to become involved in the affairs of men and remain aloof. It just isn't in our nature, Spence."

"Do you think we'll ever come back, Eustace?"

"To Hometown?"

"No, I know that's probably not likely. I just mean to Earth."

"Maybe someday."

"I'd like to see this place a year from now," said Spencer, as they passed the site of Heavenly Chalet. "I'm sure it will be all you said it would be."

"It certainly will."

"We did a good thing here, didn't we, Eustace?"

"We're ministering spirits, Spence. As such we were allowed to help."

"That's what I meant."

"I know. I guess this is far enough. Are you ready to leave?"

Spencer bent over and scooped up a handful of snow. He formed it into a snowball, then threw it as far as he could. He gave one last shiver then said, "I'm ready."

Their ascent was much like their descent had been, only in reverse. The dimness grew lighter and lighter as motion became less noticeable. Warmth flowed from the brightness, and Spencer welcomed its comfort. Already he forgot what it was to be cold. No longer encumbered by his body weight, he felt lighter than air again.

When the light became all encompassing they knew they were home. As if seeing it for the first time they were amazed at its splendor and beauty.

"It's too bad they don't know what it's like up here," Spencer said. "They'd be waiting in line to come."

"That's true, but they couldn't begin to comprehend all of this. It was like me trying to explain darkness.

You weren't able to understand something so foreign to you. So it is with them. They just have to believe it's all they've been promised it will be."

"Even so, won't they be surprised when they get here?"

"They will indeed, Spencer. Oh, they will indeed."

Eleven

The Chairman called the meeting to order, and the room became silent at once. "We have present with us two brethren who have been absent from this body. As you know, Eustace and Spencer have been to Earth on special assignment. We're here today to honor our brethren. Would you both step forward." He waited for them to comply. "Eustace, as I recall, you volunteered for this assignment, the outcome of which was most uncertain. Spencer, for whatever reason, you chose to go along. The mission was a tremendous success. We take our halos off to you." All assembled rose and did just that. "I believe that as a reward for a job well done a promotion was promised. I have here the orders for that promotion. They need only your signatures." He handed Eustace an enormously feathered pen, but he seemed hesitant to take it. "Go ahead, Brother Eustace, sign the papers."

"I don't think I can, Brother Chairman."

"What do you mean, you don't think you can?"

"It wouldn't be right."

"And why not?"

"Yes, Eustace, why not?" Spencer asked.

"Because we didn't do anything to earn a promotion."

"But these orders are stamped 'Successfully Completed.' Is there a mistake?"

"There's no mistake about the success of the assignment, Brother Chairman, it's just that we can't take credit for it. We may have had a part in it, but it was a small part."

"It was?" Spencer asked.

"Yes, it was. The real credit belongs as always to our Lord—"

"Eustace, that goes without saying. The promotion is simply a thank you for a job well done." The Vice Chairman again offered him the pen.

"—and to the good people of Hometown," Eustace continued. "It belongs to Tim, and his children, and those who weren't afraid to listen to their hearts."

"But would they have listened to their hearts if you hadn't persuaded them to do so?"

"Maybe not, but our persuasion would have been futile had they chosen to harden them."

"But they didn't," the Vice Chairman said, still holding the pen.

Spencer reached for it. "No, they didn't, Eustace."

"Spencer," said Eustace, "do you think *you* could have done anything to get Andrew Parsons to the pageant? Why, all of our celestial strength combined wouldn't have budged him. One little plea from Misty turned his heart to butter."

"Andrew Parsons? You mean he was there?"

"Yes, he was. And they'll find out one of these days."

"But what about the trade, Eustace? That was completely your doing."

"Was it, Spence? The lot by the pond was what the church really needed. I merely hinted that they could get what they wanted by giving up what they didn't. They acted on that hint—not us."

"I see what you mean." Spencer set down the pen with a sigh. "We can't sign, Brother Chairman. It wouldn't be right."

"This is highly irregular," he said, looking to the Vice Chairman.

"Highly," was all he could add.

"You're sure you want to do this?"

"We're sure."

"Well, I guess we won't need these." The Chairman tore the orders for the promotion in two.

Spencer couldn't help feeling a little disappointed. "May I keep them," he asked, "as a memento."

"You may," the Chairman replied, and the meeting was adjourned.

"Are you mad at me, Spence?" Eustace asked when The Committee members had left the chamber.

"Heavens no," he replied. "What you said was true. If anyone deserves a promotion, it's Tim and his family. And they'll get it one day. I'll be happy to see them again."

"So will I."

"If you want to know the truth, I'm really glad it worked out like it did. I'd miss The Committee."

Eustace agreed. "I don't know about you, but I'd like to get home."

"It's funny, Eustace. When we were gone it seemed as though we'd been away forever. Now that we're back I can hardly remember being gone."

"It's the dimension. Soon the sensation of time will fade away completely. Could I walk with you as far as my dwelling place?"

"Actually, I'm not leaving just yet. I want to put a few things in my locker."

"I'll come along. By the way, I want to thank you again for going with me. You made the trip most enjoyable."

"The pleasure was all mine."

In The Committee locker room an angel or two chatted with the Chairman. Eustace and Spencer offered greetings as they entered, and were received with a new level of regard.

"That was a fine thing you did," said one.

"Great job," said the other. Both patted them on the back on the way out, and Spencer knew without a doubt he and Eustace had done the right thing.

"I have to agree." The Chairman smiled with genuine approval. "Not only was it a great job, but your attitude about it is most impressive. I must confess, I had my doubts about the outcome of this mission." He offered his hand, which each gratefully accepted.

Spencer opened his locker and hung the two halves of his canceled promotion inside. Then, from his bag he took out Misty's Christmas gift, and hung it above them.

"What are those?" the Chairman asked with a curious air.

"They're wings, Brother Chairman. I'm saving them for an angel." He gave Eustace a wink, and together they headed for home.

To order additional copies of

A HEAVENLY
CHRISTMAS
IN HOMETOWN

Have your credit card ready and call

Toll free: (877) 421-READ (7323)

or send $14.99* each plus $5.95 S&H** to

WinePress Publishing
PO Box 428
Enumclaw, WA 98022

or order online at: www.winepressbooks.com

*Washington residents, add 8.4% sales tax

**add $1.50 S&H for each additional
book ordered